SHORT-TERM TRADING, LONG-TERM PROFITS

Jon Leizman, Ph.D.
with On-Site Trading, Inc.

McGraw-Hill, Inc.

New York San Francisco Washington, D.C. Auckland Bogotá
Caracas Lisbon London Madrid Mexico City Milan
Montreal New Delhi San Juan Singapore

Library of Congress Cataloging-in-Publication Data

Leizman, Jon
　　Short-term trading, long term profits/by Jon Leizman.
　　　　p.　　cm.
　　Includes bibliographical references.
　　ISBN 0-07-137520-1
　　1. Speculation. 2. Stocks. 3. Investments. I. Title.
　　HG6041 .L444　2001
　　332.63′228—dc21

2001034098

McGraw-Hill

A Division of The McGraw·Hill Companies

1 2 3 4 5 6 7 8 9 0　DOC/DOC　0 9 8 7 6 5 4 3 2 1

ISBN 0-07-137520-1

Printed and bound by R. R. Donnelley & Sons Company.

This publication is designed to provide accurate and authoritative information in regard to the subject matter covered. It is sold with the understanding that the publisher is not engaged in rendering legal, accounting or other professional service. If legal advice or other expert assistance is required, the services of a competent professional person should be sought.
　　　　　　　　　　— From a declaration of principles jointly adopted by a Committee
　　　　　　　　　　　of the American Bar Association a Committee of Publishers.

McGraw-Hill books are available at special quantity discounts to use as premiums and sales promotions, or for use in corporate training programs. For more information, please write to the Director of Special Sales, Professional Publishing, McGraw-Hill, Two Penn Plaza, New York, NY 10121-2298. Or contact your local bookstore.

 This book is printed on recycled, acid-free paper containing a minimum of 50% recycled, de-inked fiber.

For Seth and Jacob

DISCLAIMER

THIS BOOK IS DESIGNED FOR EDUCATIONAL PURPOSES ONLY. It is not designed to provide all the information required to successfully trade. Trading may involve a significantly higher level of risk in comparison to other common forms of capital management, such as long-term investments in stocks, bonds, or mutual funds. Trading may result in the loss of all of a trader's capital. The author, On-Site Trading Inc., and the publisher assume no responsibility due to, but not limited to, losses incurred as a result of applying what is discussed in this book. The author, On-Site Trading Inc., and the publisher do not claim or guarantee your success at trading or suggest that any past performance mentioned in this publication indicates the same results will occur in the future.

CONTENTS

ACKNOWLEDGMENTS

F OR THEIR HELP IN THIS PROJECT, I thank my editor Stephen Isaacs, Gary Mednick, David Kohn, Don Comrei, Phil Yee, and especially Dave Lampach.

INTRODUCTION

THE SECURITIES INDUSTRY HAS LONG BEEN a major engine of
wealth creation in the United States and around the
globe. For well over a hundred years, stockbrokers,
investment bankers, investment advisors, money managers, and traders have staked their fortunes in the
canyons of the lower Manhattan financial district. A more recent
phenomenon has been the rise of short-term trading among the
more traditional Wall Street industries.

A trader's ability to profit rests initially upon access to current
information. During the past decade, computers have leveled the
playing field, allowing inexpensive access to current information.
Faster communications equipment has permitted orders to flow in
and out at unparalleled speeds. At the same time, total market volume and volatility have risen at a dramatic pace. Consider that in
1998 the average Nasdaq daily volume was 800 million shares a day.
In 1999 that number increased to 1 billion. In the third quarter of
2000 it reached 1.58 billion.

Day Trading

By current Securities and Exchange Commission estimates, there are about 5000 professional day traders who account for approximately 15% of the Nasdaq's current volume (Figure FM-1). Traders need quality market data, reliable trade execution, and a professional environment to stimulate a successful trading mentality.

The NASD recently defined a *day trader* as "an individual who conducts intraday trading in a focused and consistent manner, with the primary goal of earning a living through profits derived from this trading strategy." The SEC further adds, "The principle characteristic that distinguishes day traders from other market participants is their mindset. Day traders generally acknowledge that they are not investors, due to the short time they hold positions. Many day traders hold stocks for seconds or hours, seldom overnight, closing out positions for small profits." The goal is to take advantage of small price movements in stocks. Minute-to-minute differences in market conditions now yield real trading opportunities. A large portion of the following pages deal with day trading and its related strategies.

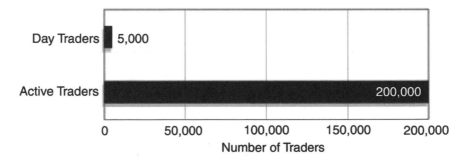

Figure FM-1.   Day trading

Alternate Short Term Trading Strategies

Day trading is only one of many short-term strategies. Some other strategies are:

Overnight trading: typically characterized by positions initiated in the last hour of a trading day, and closed in the first hour of the following session

Swing trading: a two- to five-day trade

Position trading: a trade occupying a five- to thirty-day, or longer, cycle

These methods peer beyond the momentary price movements of a stock. While day trading tends to deal solely with price action, longer-term trading utilizes a more fundamental approach, that is, general economic and market conditions, and the particular company —its products, market share, earnings, and quality of management.

A craftsman uses all tools at his disposal to create or complete a project. Likewise, a trader must have a toolbox of his or her own to meet ever changing market conditions. Knowledge of multiple trading strategies can only enhance a trader's potential for success. This book explores several short-term trading strategies in greater detail.

Technical Analysis

This book also addresses *technical analysis.* A technical analyst's main tool is the chart, a series of plotted points or bars representing months, or even years, of previous trading history. This information can include any combination of price, volume, and volatility. Many chartists perform functions on these data, yielding even more complex technical views of a stock's history. A chartist both believes a stock's past behavior is indicative of how it will trade in the future, and that patterns are recurrent. If most of a pattern is seen, it is assumed the next price movement will complete it. Head and shoulders, upright and inverted, wedges, right and left, and saucers are but a few of the patterns a technical analyst looks for. Charts are contemplated as the ancients contemplated the heavens and sought or imposed archers, goats, and bears upon the stars. Charts have historical utility. They recapitulate what has happened in a useful, easily grasped form. Their predictive value, however, is less certain, seeming to derive less from the quantifiable than from the chartist's intuition.

Psychology

While necessary, good information and fast execution are not sufficient. High technologies are worthless without a knowledgeable, focused, and committed trader correctly implementing them. A trader's mentality will ultimately prove his or her success. There are many reasons why an inexperienced trader can fail. Most of these are psychological. All traders need to follow a disciplined system. Although intuition can be a valuable tool for advanced traders, for a new trader the most important skill to develop is discipline. A section of this book deals with the psychological pitfalls a trader may encounter on the road to profitability.

Conclusions

Equity traders are not investors. A trader's profits are the result of superior timing, fast execution, and timely information, all in the context of a time horizon that is much shorter than that of an investor's. The needs and tools of a trader are very different from those of an investor.

This book does not endorse any one trading strategy. Rather, it combines the perspectives of top traders, fundamentalists (their emphasis upon value, growth, risk reduction), and technical analysts (notably their graphic summaries of history and next-step prognostication) to give the trader the flexibility to trade according to his or her objectives. One should not commit more than 20 percent of one's total capital to trading, and of that portion, no more than five percent risked on a single trade. The remaining capital should be used to develop an investment portfolio: mutual funds, bonds, municipals, and blue chips. Those are the principles of money management, which a later chapter deals with in detail.

Finally, it is important to realize that trading has the attributes of a profession. It requires tools one must learn to use; it demands discipline one must develop; and it demands time, in the order of two years of basic training, to determine if one can make a living trading stocks. Trading is inherently speculative and entails risks that are not part of investing. Trading is neither appropriate nor possible for all people. Capital can and is lost while trading, and prospective traders must be able to afford these losses without compromising their financial condition or future. Trading can be an exciting and profitable venture for those people for whom it is appropriate.

P   A   R   T   I

THE TOOLS OF
TRADING

C H A P T E R

CLASSIC INVESTMENT THEORY

AS YOU ARE PROBABLY AWARE, WHEN IT COMES to stock investing, there's no shortage of methods, strategies, plans, and theories to make money. Some are flaky, others are proven. None of them are gospel. In this section, we will introduce you to some of the best known and most effective stock investment theories.

What does this have to do with short-term trading? The answer is simple: a lot. As you will see, many long-term investment principles can be scaled down, reshaped, and modified so you can use them in your short-term trading strategies.

There are really only two kinds of trades: growth or momentum (trend) and value (countertrend). The late 1990s saw a huge surge in many momentum investors' portfolios. As prices soared, *price-earnings* (P-E) ratios (which you will learn about) reached unprecedented levels and lost meaning. Many claimed the old value-investing style, with high regard for the P-E multiple, had become meaningless. After all, many hot new economy Internet stocks had no earnings at all.

However, whenever there is the inevitable market correction, or a hot sector cools, value investors show their strength. Less spectacular than the momentum investor, slow and steady may also win the race.

In this unit you will learn the basics of value and momentum investing. These same principles can be applied on a microlevel when you begin to trade.

At the heart of any trading strategy, whether it be long-term or short-term, are sound principles of money management. You need to be careful with your money. Before entering any trading strategy or position, you must know how much you are willing to lose against your profit potential. A strategy where you are willing to lose two dollars, against a profit potential of one dollar, is doomed to failure. This is the heart and soul of all investing. What level of respect a person has for money and numbers, and the exponential effect percentages have upon them, is a major indicator as to whom the winners and losers are in the market.

As with all trading, you must allocate money at different levels. There is the level of individual allocation, as in taking a position in a stock. But there are also more macrolevels such as how much you will be short or long at any given time. Going even further, you must decide how much money you will allocate to short-term trading, versus long-term trading. We recommend allocating no more than 20 percent of your available capital to short-term trading. The rest should go into longer-term investment vehicles (i.e., mutual funds, investment stock positions, bonds, real estate, and so on). (See Figure 1-1.)

If you are a beginning trader, what you trade is going to be just as important as how you trade it. Following are three important areas you should consider before making a trade.

Diversify

You can get hurt if you put all your eggs in one basket. It's a bit cliché, but nevertheless true. This especially goes when you are

Figure 1-1. Allocation of trading money.

dealing with the world of investing. If your money is all in one sector, or concentrated in a stock or two, you are greatly exposed if that part of the market tumbles. When investing for the longer term, diversification may mean selecting stocks in different sectors or buying broader market index funds. In the short term, it may mean simply having long, strong stocks, and short, weak ones in a particular sector. Presumably, in a strong market, strong stocks should go up a great deal more than weak stocks. The opposite is true for a weak market. By eliminating some of the downside risk, you in turn eliminate some of the upside potential. The idea is to craft a scenario where your downside potential is less than your upside potential. The best offense is a good defense.

Have a Plan

It is important to have a clear objective when approaching a trade. You will find yourself in scenarios where you are unclear about what is happening with your stock, and unsure about what you want out of it. You must continually have objectives. They can at times be redefined by the changing environment, but you must be clear.

For most investors, selling is a lot harder than buying. If you've lost some money, the temptation is to stay with the stock and hope it comes back. If the stock goes up, the temptation is to stay with it and hope it will go up even more. It has been said that greed and fear move the market. These are emotions, and they are the enemy of the trader. By establishing strict parameters regarding where you will buy and sell, you remove greed and fear from the equation. Even if your parameters are incorrect, you can adjust them for future trades. Eventually you will find a system that works for you. As long as you keep emotion out of the game, it's mathematical.

Many money managers use a 20 percent rule. They use a sell limit order which is 20 percent above, and a sell stop which is 20 percent below, the price they paid for a given stock. This completely eliminates emotion, so the money managers can focus on making good picks. Under this formula, if they are correct 51 percent of the time, they are profitable. Limit and stop orders are ways to lock in profits or cut losses without agonizing over whether you should sell or buy. They automatically do the work for you.

Volatility

Beware of stocks with high volatility. These are generally stocks that trade with very low relative volume, and have prices that move in huge clips. These are the stocks that show you the money. Most recently these tended to be Internet stocks. Don't let greed draw you into high-volatility stocks.

A good measure of volatility is a stock's beta coefficient. This is simply a measure of how volatile a stock is in relation to the market. Usually, the Standard & Poor's 500 is used as the comparison index. If a stock has a beta of 1.0, it rises and falls in a one-to-one relationship with the market. If its beta is greater than 1.0, it swings much wider than the market. A beta less than 1.0 reveals movements which are more muted than an average market stock. A high or low beta is not good or bad. It's a way of determining how risky or conservative a trade will be. When buying a stock, you must be able to factor in your ability to handle risk. The beta coefficient is another tool to help you manage risk effectively.

Also, beginner traders should avoid stocks with low average daily volume. Low volume reflects price instability, market illiquidity, and high volatility. Try to avoid trading stocks with average daily volumes lower than 500,000 shares. This will make your trading career a much less painful experience.

Value Investing

Value investing is like shopping for a bargain at a flea market. The idea is to look for something that may have on it some dust, rust, or may even be badly beaten up. But, underneath the obvious defects is something you think is a treasure that may have a lot more value than the price tag states.

Value investors take that exact approach. A stock may be cheap for many reasons. The market often reacts wildly, even irrationally, to earnings that arrive under Wall Street expectations by a penny or two. Maybe economic times are bad. Maybe a company with a good product has poor management. Some companies have assets that are more valuable than the market generally assumes. It may have a marketing strategy better than Wall Streeters understand. Maybe the company has been like a sinking ship, where the captain may be thrown overboard and new management brought in.

If the new captain and his lieutenants are better than the market thinks they are, the price of the stock probably will be lower than it should be. Perhaps the company owns something, like a patent or an oil field, whose true worth is unrecognized by the market. Of course, not every cheap stock is valuable, just as not every item at a flea market is a bargain. Sometimes there's a good reason why the price is so low. Value investors try to sort out the gems from the junk.

One of the great features of value investing is that, if a stock is already beaten up and it falls even more, the low price means it won't have that far to fall—just as if you bought a beaten-up lamp at the flea market. If you were wrong, and that purchase turned out to be nothing more than an old, banged-up lamp that you had to sell at a loss, you probably would not lose much because you paid so little to begin with. If you're right, a collector will pay you a lot more than you paid at the flea market because the price was so low to start with. At least, that's the theory.

You can use these two distinct ways to try analyzing whether a battered stock is trash or treasure:

1. Where is it in the pack? This method is called relative valuation. First, you take a benchmark you think is appropriate for the stock. Maybe it's the Standard & Poor's 500. If you're looking at a technology stock, you might look at that stock's particular grouping or sector. Using that group as a basis of comparison, you decide how the stock compares to the others in terms of dividends, yield, and earnings. Is it better, worse, or just about average?

   A few definitions: *Dividends* are the amount a company pays shareholders. Dividends can be paid in quarters, semiannually, annually, or whenever the company chooses to announce. Companies usually pay them every three months. *Yield* is the rate of return on a stock as a percentage. If a stock is worth $10 and pays $1 in dividends, it has a 10 percent yield (don't hold your breath waiting for one paying that well). *Earnings* consist of how much profit a stock has, compared to the number of shares stockholders own. A stock with a $50 million profit (after taxes) and 10 million shares has earnings of $5 per share.

2. How much is the company worth—really? By taking a stem-to-stern look at the basic circumstances of the company, you decide what the stock's price actually should be. This kind of examination involves closely inspecting the earnings, assets (what the company owns and is owed), dividends, prospects for the future, and how good the management is.

Here are a few well-known value investors and approaches.

Benjamin Graham

The truly classic value investor, Graham is considered the father of modern security analysis. Graham had a knack for sniffing out bargains, and had several yardsticks for calculating whether a stock was undervalued. He also knew that his methods weren't the only ones that worked.

Graham was a broad thinker. He decided that an investor had to examine both the hard numbers and the more abstract type variables. The hard numbers included assets, liabilities (what the company owes), operating profit or loss (how much money the business has coming in, minus the costs and expenses related to the business), and capitalization (the number of shares multiplied by the price of the share).

Graham liked larger companies. He also looked for companies that had a record of paying dividends without interruption in addition to earnings growth, as well as low debt to equity. Just as important, he said, were the hard-to-quantify qualities, including what the nature of the business is, what its prospects are, the company's stability, the quality of the management, and where future earnings might be headed.

David Dreman

Graham liked the low P-E ratio as a yardstick. But a more recent P-E advocate, David Dreman, has worked on considerable research in the area. Dreman is considered a contrarian, someone who invests in stocks the market doesn't particularly like. He is author of *Contrarian Investment Strategies: The Next Generation*. Dreman has conducted numerous P-E studies that show, over varying time periods ranging from a few years to 25, that stocks with low P-E ratios consistently have higher returns than stocks with high ratios.

He also has a liking for companies whose price per share is low compared to its book value (the price per share if the company's assets were sold and its liabilities paid off), along with an affection for better-than-average dividend yields.

It's important to consider the long-term average of a company's relative P-E ratio. Over an extended period of time, companies sell for more or less than the market averages because of the risks they pose and how well the market expects them to do. Railroads and steel companies have sold below the market for some time because the market has low expectations for those industries.

For Internet companies, the expectations are quite high even though most of them are losing money, and those companies sell for prices far higher than the market.

Warren Buffett

Buffett, also known as "The Sage of Omaha," is one of the most successful investors on record. He has taken the stock of Berkshire

Hathaway, his holding company, to such heights that buying one share costs thousands of dollars.

Buffett moved from Omaha to work for Benjamin Graham in New York from 1954 to 1956. When Graham retired, Buffett moved back to Omaha, where he has lived ever since.

Buffett has some investing guidelines which seem incredibly simple and, in some ways, actually are. He doesn't fasten on yearly results. Instead, he looks at the longer-term picture, typically four to five years. He looks for return on equity as one solid measure of a company.

To get a company's return on equity, first determine its net worth (assets minus liabilities) at the beginning of an accounting period, such as a quarter (a three-month period during the year after which a company makes earnings reports to shareholders and pays a dividend). Then divide that number into the company's net income for that same quarter after the company has paid the dividends on its preferred stock (the class of stock which gets paid first but at a fixed rate and has no voting rights), but before it pays dividends to the company's common stock (the class of stock which gets paid second but which does have voting rights and gets dividends which may go up or down). The result is expressed as a percentage.

Return on equity tells stockholders how well their money is being spent. It tells whether the company is doing better or worse than in previous quarters and how well it's doing compared to businesses in its sector. Buffett likes to see a company increasing its return on equity while having very little debt.

Buffett doesn't like cash flow. Instead, he prefers what he calls owner earnings, which adds together a company's annual net income, depreciation, depletion (a special tax break for companies which take oil, gas, coal, or other minerals out of the ground), and amortization (which is generally the gradual writing off of a fixed asset, of which depreciation and depletion are a part. In addition, it includes writing off intangible assets such as copyrights, import-export licenses, and license and advertising costs) minus future capital expenditures and any working capital which might be needed. Trying to figure out which capital assets will be needed can't produce precise figures, but that's OK with Buffett.

Buffett also likes low expenses and high profit margins. To get that number, find the company's gross profit, which is the company's net sales (the company's total sales minus returns, allowances, and shipping costs). Next, subtract the costs of buying any raw materials and producing the end product. Then divide the result by the net sales.

Another measure Buffett likes is the dollar-for-dollar yardstick. For every dollar the stock goes up in price, the company's retained earnings should go up a dollar. That figure is easy to come by; it's the difference between total income and total expenses. Retained earnings is the amount the business keeps to accumulate after the dividends are paid. If the stock's price goes up more than retained earnings, that's even better.

Michael O'Higgins

O'Higgins is famous for his "Dogs of the Dow" theory, which uses the Dow Jones Industrial Average. The DJIA consists of 30 blue-chip companies deemed to be most indicative of the economy's industrial production. With only 30 stocks, the DJIA covers somewhere between 15 and 20 percent of the value of the entire stock market. As its name suggests, the DJIA largely has industrial stocks (companies that either make something or offer services, or distribute goods or services). The DJIA is the oldest stock indicator, and the one mentioned most often by your newspaper or the evening news. It has its critics, who say it's so loaded with industrials that it's unrepresentative of the economy as a whole.

The system O'Higgins uses is simplicity itself. He combs through the closing prices of the 30 Dow Jones stocks at the end of every calendar year. He looks for the 10 stocks in that group with the highest yields, which have already been calculated in the most comprehensive stock listings, such as those in the *Wall Street Journal*, the *Washington Post*, or the *New York Times*. Then he determines which 5 out of the 10 have the lowest closing prices. He then uses one of three strategies: buying equal shares of the 10 highest-yielding stocks; buying equal shares in the 5 stocks out of the 10 high-yield stocks that have the lowest closing prices; or buying a single stock, that which is the second lowest-priced stock among the 10 high-yield stocks.

The reason this strategy is a value investment is because stocks with the highest yields are signaling that they have a solid dividend but a very low price. That low price says that the stock market has, for the moment anyway, turned its back on those companies.

John Templeton

Templeton is a renowned value investor. He sold his entire group of mutual funds to what is now the Franklin-Templeton Group. He is particularly well known for venturing into foreign stocks when others considered anything beyond American borders as unworthy. Templeton has several measures he applies to determine whether he likes a stock; among them are low P-E ratios, high earnings growth rate combined with a low P-E, and escalating pretax profit margins. He likes consistent earnings rates, although gradually rising rates are considered a bonus. Other factors he considers are the extent to which the company's competitors are effective and the major challenges to the company aside from competition.

There are a couple of other value approaches.

Price-Earnings (P-E) Ratio Analysis

This measure is very popular. It consists of finding a company whose P-E ratio is low compared to others of its kind. To find the price-earnings ratio, divide the stock's current price by its earnings per share (see Figure 1-2). If a stock is selling for $35 now and its earnings last year were $7 a share, the P-E ratio would be 5 (35 ÷ 7 = 5). That means for every $1 the stock earns, investors are currently willing to pay $5. However, investors also pay for future earnings. If the same $35 stock is expected to earn $9 a share next year, then the P-E ratio would be 3.89 (35 ÷ 9 = 3.89). The idea is to find stocks with a significantly lower P-E ratio than others in its category. That category could be almost anything, from an industry group (i.e., financial stocks) to high-yield securities, or many others.

The P-E ratio has some flaws. If the company has losses, or breaks even, then there are no earnings to compute. Also, companies in a cyclical industry or which have a small capitalization are likely to

$$\text{Price-Earnings Ratio} = \frac{\text{Current Stock Price}}{\text{Earnings Per Share}}$$

Figure 1-2. Price-earnings ratio approach.

be less stable. This means that their values are too much in flux—from day to day, week to week, or month to month—for P-E ratio to be a reliable measure. Internet stocks are a breed apart. Most of them lose money, so it's impossible to compute a P-E ratio. Yet expectations are so high that, so far, they have sold for prices considerably above the market anyway.

Cashflow

Cashflow is a highly important measure of a business for investors. It's a way of determining a company's ability to pay dividends and more. Generally, cashflow is defined as the net income (the difference between how much the company sold and how much it spent that quarter) of a business, plus depreciation (an accounting method which spreads out the cost of a fixed asset over several years), plus the value of other noncash assets such as intangible assets, including copyright patents, trademarks, licenses, goodwill, and franchises.

Companies, like people, need cash to stay afloat. Companies need money to pay dividends, of course. But they also need it to pay for all the goods and services they use; for making capital improvements (things you can touch or feel, like buildings, machinery, and computers); and for paying operating costs (wages, raw materials, gas for company cars, and electricity).

Companies with a lot of debt have to pay a considerable amount in interest. If a chance materializes to buy a strategically located piece of real estate or a company that would help the company in some way, cash-strapped companies may not have the money to make the deal. Most important, perhaps, is that during hard times, the fortunes of a company with a cash cushion are likely to have a softer landing. Companies that have cash to make it through the down times are in a good position for their leadership to make clear-headed judgments and keep their enterprise afloat.

A company's strength may be gauged by analyzing surplus cashflow. This approach adds together pretax income (how much money the company takes in before it starts paying taxes) and depreciation. Then it subtracts capital expenditures, which is the money companies spend to buy or improve capital assets. Again, these are things you can lay your hands on such as computers, machinery, or buildings.

Many money managers like companies that can pay off their entire debt from free cashflow. That figure is arrived at by taking, for the current year, the amount of cash left over after taxes, then adding the sum of all the fixed assets—the company's property used in running the business but not sold off, such as furniture, machinery, and computers—which have depreciated for that year, plus other noncash expenses such as amortization and depreciation. Then subtract all capital expenditures and any increase in working capital, which is the money left over, by subtracting the liabilities from the assets.

Growth Investing

Growth investing is the other major school of investment. While value investing looks for good news in a bad news situation, growth investors look for good news which they think will only get better. They look for accelerating earnings that are ahead of the pack, and for companies whose earnings are predicted to stay ahead of the market over a long period of time. If those earnings do stay ahead of the market, so will the stock price—at least that's the way growth investors hope it works.

Peter Lynch

Lynch was one of the investing giants of the 1980s. He is arguably the person who, more than any other person in the investing field, made putting money into mutual funds exciting for Main Street investors. He accomplished that feat through a combination of legendary returns from his Fidelity Magellan Fund and a common-sense way of explaining himself that endeared him to middle-class investors.

Lynch used several strategies. He wanted the company's earnings per share to grow between 25 and 50 percent. Higher than 50 percent was too strong to be sustained, in his opinion. He also liked to examine the P-E ratio very closely. He divided the rate of growth in the company's earnings into the current P-E ratio. What is an acceptable P-E ratio? That's hard to say anymore. P-E ratios are much higher than they used to be. Perhaps the best way to decide what is an acceptable P-E ratio is by determining what the average is for that sector.

In addition, Lynch generally wanted a company's inventories to stay abreast of sales. If inventory starts to increase faster, that's a red flag. He also had some more folksy rules of thumb, such as whether he liked the store and whether the company's annual reports had a minimum of pictures in it.

Martin Zweig

Zweig's most famous accomplishment was to call the Crash of 1987 on the Friday before the crash hit. Zweig is the chairman of The Zweig Fund and the Zweig Total Return Fund, and he publishes the *Zweig Forecast*.

Zweig wants to see a company's earnings be relatively stable and have a 20 percent rise in each of the preceding three quarters. He doesn't like a company having a lot of debt. He also looks for a company's P-E ratio to be higher than five but not more than three times the current P-E for the overall market. In addition, he wants earnings growth to not be markedly higher than revenue growth, a rising sales growth in quarterly sales, and an increase in annual earnings for each of five years.

William J. O'Neil

O'Neil bought his own seat on the New York Stock Exchange at age 30 with his stock market profits, and he founded the investment firm of William O'Neil and Co., Inc., whose clients include many of the world's largest institutional investors. He also is the founder of *Investor's Business Daily*. O'Neil's approach is known by the acronym CANSLIM (C = Current quarterly earnings per share; A = Annual earnings per share; N = New; S = Shares outstanding; L = Leaders; I = Institutional sponsorship; M = The general market), which seeks earnings per share that are up at least 25 percent in the last quarter, an annual increase of 25 to 50 percent in earnings per share over a period of five years, a great new product or service that is selling very well, a major shift of some kind in the industry conditions, and less than 30 million shares of all shares outstanding. He thinks investors should learn to analyze daily price and volume charts and recognize when the market has topped or bottomed out.

Other Stock-Hunting Techniques

As we said at the beginning, there's no shortage of long-term stock-investing theories and techniques. Used judiciously, some can be quite successful. Here are a few others you should know about.

Stock Splits

Stock splits wouldn't seem to be very important. When a company splits its stock, the value of what you hold doesn't change at all. Suppose you handed a cashier a one-dollar bill and received four quarters in exchange. You're no richer or poorer than you were before. That's what a stock split is like. Handing in a dollar bill and getting four quarters back is like having a 4 for 1 stock split. However, the reason stock splits can be such a big deal is psychological in nature. Many people believe a high price means fewer people are willing to buy it, and that a lower stock price means that many more people will be willing to own that company. In concrete terms, a $150 stock is too rich for many people, but far more people would be willing to buy the same stock if it split 3 for 1 and became a $50 stock. A considerable amount of research says that a split stock's price does go up after the split, but it can and often does drift downward after that. The best advice: consider dumping the stock right after the split announcement, when the price is likely to be going up the most.

Playing Defense

When the market and the economy are failing, you don't want your portfolio to do the same. That's the time to find stocks involved in goods and services people won't do without. Even in the toughest of times, people need to eat, sleep, throw out the garbage, and see a doctor if they're sick. Some stocks, even within the areas people consider necessary to their daily life, can be of mixed worth. You want companies that don't have much debt, but do have strong revenue and earnings records, a niche market, and a good supply of cash in the bank. An investor may want to hold defensive stocks when the market sours.

When playing defense, you might consider convertible stocks or bonds, which can be swapped for a specified number of common shares at a specified price, and which pay higher dividends than common stock.

Cyclical Stocks

Investing in cyclical stocks requires a contrary streak and more patience than many investors can muster. Cyclical stocks are tied to the business cycle. When the economy is up, so are the stocks. When the economy is heading downward, so are these stocks. Examples would be autos, housing, paper, and banks. The best time to buy these stocks is during a recession, when they're cheap. But you have to be ready to play the waiting game. These stocks won't go higher until the economy regains its health.

Turnarounds

To capitalize on turnaround investments, you have to be willing to be a maverick. A turnaround situation exists when a company's stock and prospects have been sliding, but the company's fortunes are on the verge of being turned around. Although this special situation often is associated with bankruptcies, a company doesn't have to be that far gone in order to be a good turnaround candidate. There can be lots of reasons why a company has problems: too much debt, too little money, missed chances to grow, or obsolete equipment or products. Perhaps outside forces, such as a huge price hike in raw materials, are responsible.

Whatever the circumstances, the company's earnings and profits will slip and bad publicity will frighten off many investors, including mutual funds, whose investment guidelines will bar them from putting money into this situation. However, as the company's fortunes rebound, money will follow, likely raising the stock's price. In addition, if you're wrong and the stock price continues to slide, the price was already so badly battered when you bought it that hopefully it won't have much further to fall.

The classic case in this category is Chrysler. This automaker's earnings had plummeted from $5.90 a share in 1987 to losing $2.74 a share in 1991. Its share price dropped from $48 down to less than $10. Cyclical investors who correctly analyzed Chrysler's situation could have scooped up a lot of shares and would have more than doubled their investment by mid-1992, when the stock hit $21 per share.

Remember, only a few stocks in deep trouble are worth an investment. Some positive turnaround signs include a change in management, eliminating divisions, and big write-offs. Sunnier developments include discovery of a new mineral deposit, a merger or acquisition, or a strategic joint venture. Remember to focus on the biggest companies or the tiny ones with a very focused specialty. Do your homework: scour the annual reports as well as the federally required Securities and Exchange Commission reports. Read business, financial, and trade news, along with *Value Line, Morningstar,* and *S&P Outlook.* Be patient.

Total Return

For this approach, investors look for stocks which have a track record of great dividends and an ever-increasing price but which currently are having tough times. Many stocks aren't paying much if any dividends, so finding one with good dividends is a big plus. Some elements to look for are companies that consistently increase dividends and companies that buy back their own stock.

Seasonality

The ups and downs of the stock market wouldn't seem to have much predictability over the long term, or even from year to year. In fact, there are some events which happen every year when the market, generally speaking, rises or falls a lot more regularly than you'd expect.

There are several different factors which are of interest. First, the market goes up on Friday a lot more often than on any other day of the week. Second, the market seems to celebrate holidays a little early; it often goes up during the two trading sessions before most of the big ones—including Christmas, New Year's, Good Friday, the Fourth of July, and Memorial Day. Third, the last two trading days of each month and the first four of the following month generally produce an overall rise in the market.

There is even some predictability to the market during the last half of any year and the beginning of the next one. Stocks seem to go up during the summer and down during the fall. In January, sometimes the stocks of small companies go up markedly more than the stocks of larger companies. The January Effect, as it's called, does have some reasons behind it. As the end of the year approaches, institutions and individuals sell a lot of stocks for tax reasons, and mutual fund directors buy particularly good stocks as "window dressing" for their end-of-the-year portfolio. Then, in January, with those factors out of the way, the real value of stocks come into play again.

Not too surprisingly, there are stocks whose fortunes rise and fall with the seasons. The best examples are retail companies whose sales and profits naturally go up during the holidays at the end of the year, when consumers do a large percentage of their retail buying for the entire year. The end-of-the-year holiday season is also a time when stocks usually rise. Some people think it's just the good feelings people have during that time. More likely, though, is the fundamental fact that corporations contribute to pension or profit-sharing plans during that time, and much of that money goes into stocks.

One way to keep track of seasonality trends is to read Yale Hirsch's "Stock Trader's Almanac," a yearly report on seasonality.

Dow Theory

Charles H. Dow developed this theory from 1900 to 1902, when he was the *Wall Street Journal* editor. Dow said that the market has three kinds of trends: major, which endure for a couple of months to several years; intermediate, which lasts from a couple of weeks to several months; and minor, which go for a few days up to a few weeks. To confirm whether a market move does fall into one of these categories, Dow said that the Dow Jones Industrial Average and the Dow Jones Transportation Average both had to reach new highs or lows.

Index Funds

One of the easiest and most stress-free ways to invest your money is to purchase index mutual funds. Basically, an index fund is run by a computer which chooses stocks only on the basis of producing returns precisely the same as the particular index to which it's pegged. The advantage: most funds run by money managers don't match their indices, let alone beat them.

There are a number of indices. The most commonly used one is the Standard & Poor's 500 (S&P 500), which includes 500 of the largest and most profitable companies in the United States. If you invest in the S&P 500 index fund, your returns will be almost the same as the index itself. If the index goes up 13 percent—a fairly common average yearly return over the long term for this index— then that fund will go up the same amount. If it goes down 13 percent, so does your money. The fund generates these returns because all the investing is done by a computer programmed to match the index, not by managers trying to outsmart the market by speculating about what turn the market will take tomorrow or next week, and which stocks will be going up or down.

However, a fund will always return slightly less than the index does. This is because mutual funds, no matter how automated, have expenses. Just make sure to purchase an index fund with low expenses, usually under 1 percent. Low expense is only one indexing advantage. Others include lower portfolio turnover, which produces lower trading commissions. And, because an index fund reflects the whole index, it's far more diversified than most managed funds.

Some other commonly used indices include the S&P Midcap (medium-sized companies), the Russell 2000 (smaller companies), and the Wilshire 5000 (the entire market).

What you've read here is a rapid tour of some classic investment styles and approaches. No matter which ones you use, be sure to keep up with the market. Read the *Wall Street Journal*, *Investor's Business Daily*, *Barron's*, the trade press of whatever business a company is part of, *Value Line*, and anything else you can find. Picking good stocks, whether for the short term or the long, requires a lot of information and the willingness to use your knowledge to advantage. Stock picking is hard work. Done well and consistently, it can pay you handsome rewards.

Classic Investment Theory Review Questions

Choose the corresponding letter. A letter can be used more than once.

1. January Effect
2. Relative Valuation
3. Dogs of the Dow
4. Stock Trader's Almanac
5. Convertible Stocks and Bonds
6. Accelerating Earnings
7. Bankrupt Companies
8. Benjamin Graham
9. Housing, Paper Stocks
10. Peter Lynch

A. Cyclical Investing
B. Growth Investing
C. Seasonality Investing
D. Defensive Investing
E. Value Investing
F. Turnaround Investing

Classics Investment Theory Review Answers

1. C
2. E
3. E
4. C
5. D
6. B
7. F
8. E
9. A
10. B

CHAPTER

2

TRADING BASICS

DON'T ASSUME YOU HAVE ALL THE KNOWLEDGE you'll need to sit down in front of a computer screen and start trading stocks. We want you to have all the knowledge needed to craft your own individual trading style, and to be successful at it.

The most fundamental question, which is not asked often enough, is this: What, exactly, is stock? *Stock* represents ownership in a company. Each *stockholder* has at least one share of the company's outstanding stock. A *share* is a unit of ownership. You might own one share or 10,000. However many shares you own, each share has a claim on the assets and earnings of that company.

Having stock in a company, even if you hold only one share, means that you own a piece of it. You are, in fact, an owner even though you have nothing to do with the day-to-day decisions of the company. There are several different kinds of stock. You'll be most interested in *common stock*, which is the stock of choice for traders. Because of the nature of common stock, it's where most of the action is. Much of the discussion in this book pertains to common stock, which has several key features.

Common Stock

1. If the company is paying dividends, every share of common stock will pay one. A *dividend* is a payout for each share authorized by the board of directors and usually is paid every quarter, or every three months in the calendar year (March, June, September, December). Dividends can be paid at any interval, in fact, whenever the board of directors deems them appropriate. Some companies don't pay dividends on their common stock. The risk for the common shareholder is that common stock dividends are unpredictable, and can even be stopped altogether.

2. Each share of common stock carries one vote. Common stockholders get to vote on matters such as who gets to sit on the board of directors, and on policy matters ranging from an antidiscrimination pronouncement to which top executives get stock options and how much.

3. If a company has growth, the common shares will tend to reflect greatly inflated prices in relation to the company's book value. The rewards are highest for common stockholders of a successful company. However, where rewards are high, risks tend to be high as well. So, when the company goes bankrupt, everybody else gets paid before the holders of common stock. That's just part of the risk of common stock ownership.

Preferred Shares

You may want to trade in other kinds of shares besides common stock, so here is a little information about preferred stock. Although there are several different kinds of preferred stock, they all have some features in common:

1. They all pay a more predictable dividend than the same company's common stock pays.

2. What makes this stock preferred is that holders of this kind of stock get their dividends before holders of common stock. However, preferred stock doesn't guarantee a dividend, only that you'll get one if the company is paying one.

3. If a company stops paying dividends for some reason, then the dividends that would have been paid to holders of preferred

stock accumulate. If the company resumes paying dividends, the holders of preferred stock have to be paid the money that has piled up in their dividend backlog before common stockholders are paid any new dividends. Common stock does not accumulate any dividend backlog.

4. Preferred stockholders usually don't have voting rights. They can't vote on who gets to sit on the board of directors or other matters.

These features make preferred stock a safer investment than common stocks, which means market conditions and investor sentiment have less effect on the preferred stock's price than on the price of common stock. The result: Preferred stock is less volatile and has fewer big price swings, so traders have fewer opportunities to make money.

Dividends

You should know that dividends, or the lack of them, are an important indicator of the nature of the stock. *Growth stocks* are companies that skip paying dividends so they can instead put the money into stoking their expansion. The companies fitting this definition would include many of the technology stocks such as Microsoft or Dell.

Bluechip stocks usually have a strong record of paying out dividends each quarter and generally increasing their dividends over the years as well. Active traders generally ignore this factor because traders don't intend to be in a stock long enough to collect dividends.

Valuation

Before diving into the world of common stocks, you should know how they are valued. Here are three different varieties of valuation:

1. **Par:**   Par value is a number almost plucked out of the air. It's an arbitrary dollar amount assigned to a company's stock when it incorporates. Although you will hear this term occasionally, it has no practical use for a trader.

2. **Book:**   This dollar figure is the amount each share would be worth if the company's assets were sold and its liabilities paid off. It's a rough approximation of what a company would be worth if it were liquidated. A company which would have $50 million cash in hand after all its assets were sold and debts paid, and which had 10 million shares outstanding (held by shareholders), would have a book value of $5 a share.

   Be careful when looking at book value, because different kinds of companies tend to have different kinds of book values. The worth of service companies is determined largely by what people do for customers. Such a company won't have a lot of equipment or property to sell. These companies generally have lower book values. Manufacturing companies have lots of equipment and other material on hand which could be sold off, so their book values generally are higher.

3. **Market:**   This is the most important figure to a trader. It comes down to the basic laws of supply and demand. How many potential stockholders want it, and how much is available to be bought? There's no direct relationship here between market and book values. The market value, which is how much a share of a given company sells for at a given point in time, depends largely on perception: how much investors think the stock is worth. Sometimes the stocks of great companies have a low market value for reasons having little to do with how good the company actually is. On the flip side, poorly performing companies can have high market values per share just because investors think the company is a good buy.

Trading and the Exchanges

Stock trading doesn't happen by accident. Like many other commodities, stocks have centralized organizations that try to make sure that trades happen in a smooth, orderly fashion. There are four markets. You have access to them all, as do banks, mutual funds, pension fund managers, brokers, and dealers. Brokers or dealers are middlemen, people who perform the actual transaction of buying or selling, but only at the direction of their customers or for their own corporate accounts. Here are the four major kinds of markets.

First Market

The exchange market. Exchanges are physical locations where listed stocks are bought and sold. The best-known exchange, of course, is the New York Stock Exchange. The exchanges deal in listed securities, which are securities that have been accepted for trading by one of these exchanges and are listed there. Generally, stocks you'll find on the exchanges are the larger companies such as General Electric, IBM, or Merck. These companies have a large capitalization (the number of shares in the marketplace multiplied by the price of each share), usually more than $5 billion.

Second Market

Over-the-counter market. Here is where you can trade stocks that are not listed on any of the exchanges.

Third Market

Over-the-counter listed market. Where institutions such as banks, pension managers, labor unions, corporate profit-sharing plans, and other institutional investors trade exchange-listed securities, usually in large blocks of stock; perhaps 10,000 shares and up.

Fourth Market

Here is where over-the-counter trading happens between institutional investors. This trading usually is done through Instinet, about which you'll learn more later. As a trader, you will be focusing here on two main markets: the New York Stock Exchange and the Nasdaq exchange. They have different histories, operate differently, and have different advantages.

The New York Stock Exchange

First, consider the New York Stock Exchange. It has the most prestige and is the most well-known among the various stock markets.

It's also one of the oldest. Stock trading began in this country in the late 1700s. Quickly, merchants and brokers were gathering on Wall Street to trade. In 1792 a version of the exchange had formed, although the exchange didn't take on its present form until 1817.

It's called an auction market, or an *open outcry market*, because the trading actually happens when members of the exchange call out their orders on the floor of the exchange.

It has one specific, physical location in which all the orders are executed. All stocks on the exchange are bought and sold at a designated trading post, a specific location at which a specialist in a specific stock and the crowd of traders who want to buy and sell that stock will gather.

The *specialists* have three duties: First, they act as brokers. If someone wants to place an order higher or lower than the stock market is offering at the moment, they can leave that order with the specialist. That order is entered in the book, which is the specialist's list of unexecuted orders. Although the book used to be an actual printed volume, it now consists of several flat-screen computers.

Of course, the specialists have to execute an order as the market comes to that order's price. If you wanted to sell a stock at $85, and the market was only offering $80, that order would be left in the book until a buy order at $85 came in.

The specialists' second duty is to act as an auctioneer. Whenever a broker or trader asks for a market, the specialist has to provide it. A market is a stock quotation with both a bid and an ask price. A bid is the highest amount a buyer is willing to pay, and an ask price is the lowest amount a seller will accept. For example, the bid price for IBM might be 103, and the ask price might be $103\frac{1}{2}$. The stock quotation for IBM would be 103 to $103\frac{1}{2}$. The spread, or difference between the two, would be $\frac{1}{2}$.

Often, the specialist will include his or her own bids in order to ensure there is plenty of market depth, or competition for a stock. In the course of a day, if a stock goes down strongly and no buyers are coming in, and the specialist doesn't step in as a buyer, then there's a good chance the price of the stock will go into a free fall. It becomes the obligation of the specialists to buy the stock with their own money to keep the price from sliding downward in an irrational fashion. If the stock keeps rising and there are no sellers, then the specialists must sell from their own inventory of the stock in order to supply the demand.

The specialists' third responsibility is to maintain an orderly market. That is a market where prices don't gyrate too wildly. An exchange stock is expected to trade from one price to the next without jumping over too many fractions. A stock selling for $24^5/_{16}$ shouldn't be rocketing to $25^1/_2$ without a few stops in between, such as $24^7/_{16}$, $24^{11}/_{16}$, $24^{15}/_{16}$, $25^1/_8$, $25^3/_8$, then $25^1/_2$.

To maintain an orderly market, specialists become dealers, buying for their own account. If too many sell orders materialize, the specialist must buy the stock out of his or her own money in order to put brakes on the price fall. If a stock is steaming too high, the specialist is expected to sell his or her own supply of the stock at lower prices, to take the momentum out of the rising price.

Although it would seem that the specialists might get rich at the expense of other investors—after all, they get to look at every order to buy and sell a particular stock and they are the only institutional brake or accelerator on their specific stocks—in fact, the specialists seldom trade. Their buys and sells account for about 10 percent of all trading. Usually, they simply match an order from a nonexchange member such as an individual or a bank or mutual fund to buy with another order to sell.

The Crowd are the people who bring, buy, and sell orders to the specialist. The most important members of the crowd are the floor brokers, who represent the various brokerage houses that belong to the NYSE and who bring the buy and sell orders to the specialist. The prime directive for the floor broker is to get the best possible price from the specialist for the orders the floor broker receives. Increasingly, however, many trades are being sent electronically, eliminating the need for floor brokers.

The floor broker and the specialist convene at a designated location called a trading post. About 17 of them are sprinkled around the floor of the NYSE. In essence, they're a horseshoe-shaped counter from which the specialists keep track of trading activity in their designated stocks while keeping the electronic book of buy and sell orders. A clerk stands inside the post to tell the specialist about trades and help monitor the activity. Brokers and traders, interested in buying or selling a stock, crowd around at the counter to communicate with the specialist. As a rule of thumb, the larger the capitalization of the stock, the larger the crowd around the specialist.

How do trades occur? The obvious answer is that trades happen when a buyer and seller agree on a price. It's the specialist's function to match buyers and sellers. However, you may not be able to buy or sell a stock at the price you want.

First, you need to find out what the stock quotation is on your stock. Let's say Merrill Lynch wanted to buy 1,000 shares of Merck at 80 and the A.G. Edwards brokerage house wanted to sell 3,000 Merck shares at $80\frac{1}{2}$. If no other traders want to buy or sell between those two prices, then the quote for Merck at that point would be 80 to $80\frac{1}{2}$.

If you had Merck stock, you could offer to sell it lower, say $80\frac{1}{4}$, a quarter of a point beneath the $80\frac{1}{2}$ price tag A.G. Edwards has put on it, and see if someone would buy it. If you wanted to buy the stock, you could offer to pay the $80\frac{1}{2}$ that A.G. Edwards is asking. You don't have to buy or sell the same amount of Merck stock that A. G. Edwards is offering to sell or Merrill Lynch is willing to buy. You can buy or sell as much or as little as you want and can afford.

Remember, it is the specialist who will be quoting the price, and when that price is quoted, the specialist is absolutely expected to honor that price. No bluffing here. It's put up or shut up—a key difference from the Nasdaq system, which you'll visit at much closer range in a moment.

Once two parties agree to the buying and selling of a block of stock, there are two ways in which the order is processed: either by phone or electronically, through what is called the SuperDOT system. If you're buying by phone, you'll call your broker and say you want to buy, for example, 300 shares of America Online. Then your broker phones the trading desk of his or her brokerage, where traders then call NYSE clerks who write the order and give it to a floor broker.

The floor broker heads for the correct post, the one where that specific stock is traded, and asks for a quote for the stock. If the order is in the vicinity of the quote, then the floor broker reads the order to the crowd, where somebody, or perhaps nobody, might accept the order.

If the two or more floor brokers enter the crowd with the same offer, the specialist has a list of priorities which is based on who gets the trade. Whoever submits the first order gets first priority. If they both submit at the same time, then whoever submits the largest order gets the bid. And if that's a tie, then there's a random drawing or coin flip between the competing brokers.

If the order is accepted, the floor broker returns to the clerk with the completed order. The clerk phones the traders, who tell the broker, who then phones you, the client. If the order isn't accepted, then the floor broker leaves the order with the specialist, who enters the order and executes it—if and when the stock trades at that price.

The SuperDOT electronic system peels away many layers of that system. When you ask your broker to buy the 300 shares of IBM at 100, your broker may submit the order electronically through SuperDOT directly to the specialist, who receives the order in his or her book. When the order is executed, the specialist presses a button, and your broker is told electronically that the trade has occurred. Then your broker calls you.

The Over-the-Counter Market (OTC)

This electronic market is much different than the exchange markets. The biggest one is known as the *National Association of Securities Dealers Automated Quotation* (Nasdaq).

The *National Association of Securities Dealers* (NASD) was begun in 1949, just after the federal Maloney Act was signed into law, allowing for the development of self-regulatory organizations. In 1961, the U.S. Congress told the Securities and Exchange Commission (the federal agency created in 1934 to regulate American financial markets, brokers, dealers, and almost any other people and companies connected to investing) to report on the over-the-counter market. The study, released in 1963, showed that the OTC was highly fragmented and very hard to understand. The SEC's solution: automate the system and have the NASD put that system into action. By 1971, the Nasdaq system was complete—and it now has the second-highest dollar volume of the world's stock markets.

The Nasdaq system is quite a different species from the NYSE and other exchanges. Here are some of the crucial ways in which Nasdaq differs:

- It has no centralized location. It exists only on computer screens and telephones. It's a purely electronic system in which trading is done through a highly sophisticated network which puts buyers and sellers around the world in touch with each other.

■ Nasdaq has no specialist who handles all the transactions in a given stock. Instead, brokers and dealers are the main participants. Some of these brokers and dealers are registered with Nasdaq as *market makers* in a particular stock. Market makers buy for their own account, rather than arrange for trades, as the NYSE specialists do. The market makers draw from their own inventory in a stock to buy or sell to a customer.

To be market makers, they have to be willing to offer firm prices in the stock and ready to execute those prices through buying or selling round lots (lots whose numbers are divisible by 100, such as 100, 800, and 2000 shares). The market makers have to announce their quotes through the Nasdaq system.

Each market maker operates completely independently of the others and doesn't know what the other market makers are doing. They know only what their own order flow is. Market makers compete for customers. The more orders they have, the more they can earn money on their trades and the more liquidity, or ease of buying and selling rapidly and in bulk, they will have. They have to strike a balance: they want to give their customers good prices but they also want to make money on their trades.

As a trader, you should keep an eye on the *Volume-Weighted Average Price* (VWAP). It's the average price at which the largest volume of stock for any given issue was traded during that day. That's the price that traders have to beat in order to keep their large customers, such as banks and pension funds, happy.

■ The Nasdaq is called a "negotiated market" because trades are negotiated between the buyers and sellers directly, without the middlemen such as the specialists and floor brokers.

■ Generally, the more established companies will be on the exchanges, and the younger and more technologically based companies will be on the Nasdaq. The result: the stocks of Nasdaq companies tend to be a lot more volatile than shares of companies listed on the NYSE.

Let's look at the differences between the NYSE and the Nasdaq markets that we've touched upon so far:

A. The NYSE is located in a physical space. Specific stocks are traded in specific locations in the exchange building. The Nasdaq is not located in any physical space. There's no building with Nasdaq Exchange on the directory. It's a telephone and computer system linking buyers and sellers, usually brokers and dealers.

B. The NYSE uses specialists in each stock to keep orders flowing and prices from getting out of control. These specialists occasionally buy or sell stocks out of their own inventory, but far more frequently they match buyers and sellers. The Nasdaq uses market makers, independent dealers and brokers who execute buy and sell orders and keep the market orderly through buying and selling from their own accounts.

C. NYSE buy and sell orders are auctioned to the crowd gathered at the appropriate trading post on the NYSE building floor. Nasdaq buy and sell orders are negotiated between market makers and buyers and sellers.

Order Types and Routing Systems

There are other important features you need to learn about the NYSE and Nasdaq markets. One is the various kinds of orders you can place, the other is how to get your orders where they need to go.

Before you learn how to execute orders and what execution systems are available, you need to read and consider carefully the following:

Beginning traders are in too much of a hurry to make money. Our markets have become like casinos with funds, corporations, and individuals pouring tremendous amounts of money into them, and pulling it out just as quickly. This creates a lot of short-term volatility. While experienced traders revel in high volatility, it makes quick work of the novice. The markets are similar to the myth of the American dream at the turn of the century, seeming like the land of opportunity, where the streets are paved with gold. People believe trading is a way to make a lot of money quickly. They hear stories of fortunes being made. Very few realize that the wealth has taken the trader many years to accumulate and could be lost in a few months. They think it must be simple. It is not.

Successful traders endure. Experience ultimately makes a good trader. Months or years of repetition of screen time, analyzing charts, news, and prices are required. Often a trader's best trades occur when he or she sees or intuits similar trading scenarios and trades accordingly. A strong trading strategy and system, encompassing humility, a quick mind, and hard work, are all important aspects of trading. But a trader needs to take time to develop the discipline. Initial strategies must be devised to preserve capital while gaining the necessary experience.

We want to emphasize this fact: becoming successful at trading could take you 1 to 2 years. Until you get good, don't try to get rich. Focus on not going broke. You want to have enough money left so that when you actually have the knowledge to trade well, you can afford to do it right.

Successful Trading

We want to help you hang on to your money and not go broke. Toward that end, here are some Dos and Don'ts for novice traders:

The Dos

1. Do trade only 100 to 300 shares to start. Almost all traders, even the superstars, lose at the beginning. Be prepared for those losses, and don't put down all your capital on just a few stocks. Instead, try to stay in the game. Look at trading as a profession, not just a glamorous hobby. Learning a profession, like most other good things in life, requires hard work and discipline. Develop consistency. Make sure you have the money to put all those hard-earned lessons to work.

2. Do start your trading with listed NYSE stocks and the big, brand-name Nasdaq stocks such as Microsoft, Intel, and Cisco. It's much easier to get in and out because there's more liquidity. That fact makes limiting losses a lot easier.

3. Do pick stocks with a low price-earnings ratio. Earnings consist of how much profit a stock has compared to the number of shares stockholders own. A stock with a $50 million profit (after taxes) and 10 million shares has earnings of $5 per share.

To find the price-earnings ratio, divide the stock's current price by its earnings per share. If a stock is selling for $35 now and its earnings last year were $7 a share, the P-E ratio would be 5 (35 ÷ 7 = 5). That means for every $1 the stock earns, investors are currently willing to pay $5. However, investors also pay for future earnings. If the same $35 stock is expected to earn $9 a share next year, then the P-E ratio would be 3.89 (35 ÷ 9 = 3.89).

The idea is to find stocks with a significantly lower P-E ratio than the market or than others in its category. That category could be almost anything, from an industry group (for example, financial stocks) to high-yield securities.

4. Do deal in stocks with a high float. A *float* is the number of shares outstanding and available to the public. A high float would be at least 25 million. Also, buying and selling stocks with a high daily trading volume would mean an average of at least 500,000 shares traded every day. These stocks will be easy to buy and sell and you won't have to wait.

5. Do work with stocks that have a tight spread, which is a small difference between the bid and the offer price. A tight spread for these purposes would be ¼ of a point or less. Such stocks will limit your losses because if you're on the wrong side of a trade, you can get out with a smaller loss.

6. Do work with stocks in the under-$100 price range. They're less volatile. Usually the cheaper a stock is, the less volatile it is. Because the under-$100 stocks move more slowly, you, as a beginning trader, can keep track of their movements much more easily than any of the stocks that have huge price or other technical swings. You might initially look to trade stocks in the $20 to $60 range.

7. Do trade only those stocks with volatility befitting both how much you're willing to risk and your experience. Don't try to take on the extremely volatile stocks before you're ready. They'll eat you alive.

If you don't know how to handle volatility, you can be right about a stock and still lose money. If you buy a stock at 100 and your stop is at 90, the stock could go to 105, then down to 88. At that point, your stop at 90 has just sold the stock. If the stock then goes up to 125, you were right about the stock going up, but you no longer own it. You're trading a stock too volatile for your risk parameters or your experience.

The Don'ts

Now, here are the don'ts, traps that will get you into very deep trouble if you fall into them:

1. Don't be arrogant. Don't have a need to be right. As a trader, you need to be humble and confident at the same time. New traders often believe they're right and the market is wrong, and if they just persist, the market will have to come around to seeing it their way. No, it doesn't. The market will do what it's going to do, whether you like it or not.

   Traders often don't want to admit they are wrong. That's a fatal mistake. If you are wrong, admit it and move on. Traders need confidence, but not arrogance. Even the best traders have terrible days, weeks, even months. Any trade, no matter how good it looks, can go sour. If you can't admit you're wrong, you're going to stick with losing positions far too long. That's a sure-fire way to lose your bankroll.

2. Don't assume the stock market will keep going up. Just because the market has gone up 50 to 80 percent a year in some sectors for the last few years doesn't mean it will continue to climb ever upward. You've been spoiled by the stock market's success during the last decade or so. The real test for traders is a bear market—and you had better be prepared to deal with one when it happens. Nobody knows when it's coming, but rest assured, it is coming.

3. Don't think you won't need a plan. You will. A trader without a plan is like a ship without a rudder. And if you can't steer your own ship, eventually it will be ripped open by some hazards you could have avoided but didn't. There are plenty of very successful traders who are right less than half the time, but they get out of bad positions with small losses because they have a plan and get out when they should. That's why they make a lot of money.

4. Don't bank on the current high-flying sector as the golden path to riches. For beginning traders, these are likely to be too volatile, too tricky, too treacherous. Don't trade them.

Why do people make these mistakes? Because they're at a computer, and now they, not a professional money manager, are handling their own money. One click can destroy your entire financial future. Some people don't realize the power of this situation, and they must. This is your money, not a video game. You feel all-powerful at that computer terminal, and you're not. This power is more than some people can handle.

If you can learn to avoid losing money, eventually you will have a chance to make a lot of money trading. By breaking even, you will be learning to eliminate a lot of mistakes early. When you reach a point where you don't lose money for a few months, then you are starting to learn how to make money as a trader. The equation is this simple: not losing a lot of money = eventually making money. Follow that simple formula and you have a chance to make very big money indeed.

Make a copy of all these rules, then tape them to your computer monitor, your refrigerator, and your bathroom wall. They will keep you sane, save you money, and help to keep you in the game. When you make mistakes, come back and read these warnings again.

Types of Orders

You need to know about three kinds of orders. The ones which will keep you in the game are the limit order and the stop order. First, take a look at those two, because they will help to keep fear, greed, and anxiety from paralyzing you:

Limit Order.   A *limit order* puts a cap on the price at which you're willing to buy or sell a stock. If you said you wanted to place a limit order to sell 200 shares of Motorola at $25, those shares wouldn't be sold until the price reached no less than $25. If you had a limit order to buy 200 shares of Motorola at $25, then the order wouldn't be executed until the price was no more than $25.

Here's the scoop on limit orders: There is no guarantee that your order will be filled. Limit orders are on a first-come, first-served basis. Suppose you put in a limit order to buy a stock at $99 or below, and there are orders for 10,000 shares of that stock which others have placed ahead of you in the specialist's book. If the stock dips to 99 and the specialist sells the 10,000 shares before the price starts shooting up, then your order doesn't get

filled. And if the price never gets down to 99 again, your order won't ever be filled.

Beginning traders run into this problem all the time. They think the specialist has cheated them. Almost always, that's not the case. The problem is that they were next in line to get their ticket punched when the ticket window closed.

Here are two trading tips for the times to use limit orders:

1. When things are going well for you. If you bought the stock at 100 and it's going up, you might want to sell half of it at 102. You would be using two strategies here. One is *lightening your position*, when you sell some of your stock in a company, but keep some of it, too. The second strategy is *selling into strength*. That's when you're basically figuring that the stock's upward movement has got enough gas to get it to a specific price which will give you a nice profit on the part you do sell.

   Don't get greedy and figure you'll be able to predict when the stock will hit its top price. Nobody can pick a top, and you'll lose a lot of money if you think you've got that special talent nobody else has got.

2. When you want to pick a good spot to get into a stock. If a stock is trading within a range, say between 95 and 105, and it's been doing that for a couple of days, a week, or a month, you might want to put in a limit order to buy at 96, the bottom of the range. That way, you won't have to watch the stock for days or weeks or months, but your money will be automatically ready to pounce when the stock gets to the price you want. This is a good, low-risk trade.

Stop Order.   Stop orders are most often used when you want to make sure you limit your losses or preserve your profits. They are the smart trader's insurance policy. A stop order is an order to buy or sell at whatever the market price may be after the price has reached a certain point. For example, if you wanted to place a stop order to buy 300 shares of General Electric at $75, then the stock would be bought at whatever the market price would be after the price has reached $75.

Stops also are used for selling, their most important use. If you bought 300 shares of IBM at 70 and put in a stop order to sell at 68, then you would be making sure that if the price went down from the $70 price where you bought it, you would lose only $2 a share.

Stops are essential to a trader's strategy. Here is the most essential point about buying a stock: always know at what point above and below your buying price you will sell the stock. As soon as you buy a stock, put in a sell limit to sell at whatever profit above your purchase price is acceptable to you. At the same time, also put in a sell stop for whatever loss you are willing to take.

You must use stops on every stock you buy. It's part of the discipline. Buying is easy. Selling is one of the hardest parts of the discipline to master. Before you buy any stock, you must know how far above and below the price you paid for it you are willing to sell your position.

Incidentally, there are two other ways you can use stops. To make sure you'll have a profit on a stock which is going well for you, use a trailing stop. If you bought a stock at 100 and it hits 105, you could put a stop at 102. That way, even if the stock drops, you'll assure yourself an approximately $2-per-share profit.

Another way to use stops is to be ready when a stock breaks out of a trading range. If a stock has been moving within a range of, say, 100 to 105, and you think that if the price breaks out of the top of that range it will pick up steam, you could put in a buy stop order for a price slightly above the high end of that range, say 105 1/2.

Market Order. No specific price is set. Using a *market order* means you buy the stock for whatever price is available. You may or may not like the price you get. Try not to use market orders unless they're part of a stop order, or unless you must quickly get out of a position in a fast-moving market.

The most common time to use a market order is in a market moving too fast to try to determine a price, or when you're dealing with a stock which can be bought or sold easily and is moving in a narrow range, stocks such as Coca Cola or Compaq. In that case, you likely will get a good price and fast execution.

Here is a major drawback to a market order: using a market order by itself allows room for emotion, and that's not good. Trading is a discipline. A market order might be submitted out of panic, especially when you're considering a sale. Generally speaking, use them sparingly.

The crucial differences between a limit, stop, and market order: with a limit order, you are guaranteed you will get your price or better if the order goes through—but there's no guarantee that the order will be filled, even if the market reaches the minimum price you've set.

With a stop order, if the market reaches your minimum price, then you are guaranteed that your order will be filled. However, because your order becomes a market order, you may get a worse price by the time the order is filled, but it should be in the vicinity of the stop price.

Orders: Differences between NYSE and Nasdaq

The differences between orders you can use in the two markets is simple to describe, but, as you will see, they have profound effects on how you have to approach your trading. On the Nasdaq, you can't place stop orders, and there are very few chances to do market orders. For the most part, you will be forced to use limit orders when you trade on Nasdaq. If you're going to trade on the Nasdaq, use mental stops, prices that you keep in your mind (or on paper) at which you will buy or sell each stock. Incidentally, you'll be in good company. Fund managers do not use stops in any market, so they all use mental stops, too.

Orders Entered Above the Market Price

Now that you've got the three basic types of orders in mind, here are the two kinds of orders you might use when you're aiming above the market price.

Buy Stop.   A buy stop order is above the market price. When the price reaches your target, your order becomes a market order (Figure 2-1). Your order will be filled, but, because there's no way of knowing how many orders are ahead of you and how fast the price of the stock will move or in what direction, there's no way of telling what price you'll actually pay.

If you put in a buy stop for 300 shares at 103, as soon as the market price reaches 103, your order will be filled at the market.

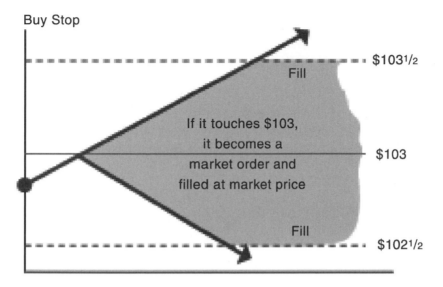

Figure 2-1. A buy stop order.

Whatever the price is when it's your order's turn to be filled, that's what you'll pay.

Sell Limit. If you put a sell limit order on 300 shares of stock now selling at the market at 100, and you want it filled at 103, then you may or may not get your wish. Your stock will be sold at 103 or higher if the market reaches the 103 mark, and then if, and only if, the stock holds that price or higher while the specialist fills the sell limit orders which have been placed ahead of yours (Figure 2-2).

Market orders are, of course, entered at the market.

Orders Entered Below the Market Price

Buy Limit. If the market has a $100 price on that stock you've been aching to buy, and you put in a buy limit order for 300 shares at 97, then the specialist can fill the order only when it's your order's turn to be filled and the price is 97 or cheaper (Figure 2-3).

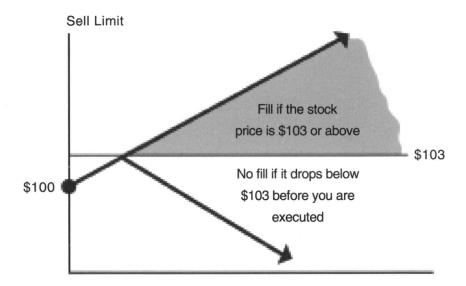

Figure 2-2. A sell limit order.

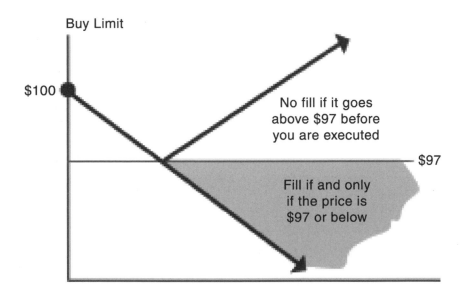

Figure 2-3. A buy limit order.

Sell Stop. If you buy those 300 shares at 103, and you put in a sell stop at 100, then as soon as the market price reaches 100, your order will be filled, but only at the market price (Figure 2-4).

Other Order Types

Here are a couple more kinds of orders you can combine with limit, stop, and market orders:

Market on open (MOO). These are executed as market orders when the market opens.

Market on close (MOC). These are executed as market orders at the market's close. Must be entered by 3:40 P.M.

Good 'til cancelled (GTC). This means that the trade is still alive until you say differently. In practice, that means 30 to 60 days. Ask your broker what the house rules are. Be sure to renew these orders when they expire. This technique is a way to keep stops alive.

Day only. This means your order is good only for the remainder of the trading day after you place it.

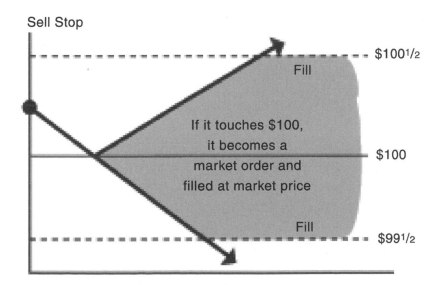

Figure 2-4. A sell stop order.

All or none (AON).   If you order more than one round lot (100 shares) to be bought or sold, you can ask that all of the lots be bought or sold or, if that doesn't happen, that none will be. The order doesn't have to be filled immediately. However, enough demand to buy or sell all of the shares you want may not materialize. If not, then you have sold no shares.

If you put all-or-none restrictions on an order, your order goes to the back of the line. Specialists will first execute other orders that don't have those restrictions. For that reason, a lot of traders find that an AON order isn't very useful. It's better to get filled for a piece of your order than to have nothing filled at all.

Immediate or cancel.   Basically what it says is what you think it says. It tells the specialist that if he or she can't fill the order as soon as it arrives, then scrub it. However, the whole order doesn't have to be filled. If only part of it can be, then the unfilled part is cancelled.

Fill or kill.   Either the complete order is filled on the first attempt or the order is canceled. There is no second attempt to execute.

Routing Systems

Your orders must have some way to get where they're supposed to go. There are several of these pathways, or routing systems. Some involve the NYSE, others involve Nasdaq.

NYSE.   The system called *SuperDOT* (Designated Order Turn-around) involves NYSE orders only, not Nasdaq. It electronically routes orders to the specialist's desk from member firms, or to the booth of NYSE brokers and dealers who give the order to a floor broker to take to auction. Usually the order goes straight to the specialist's book, never passing through the hands of floor brokers. The SuperDOT system, which can process orders of up to 99,999 shares, handles about 90 percent of the exchange's orders, accounting for about 45 percent of the shares traded.

When a SuperDOT order is given to the specialist, an assistant enters it into the Display Book, the workstation where all incoming market orders and limit orders are tracked. The specialist can execute the order by matching a buyer with a seller in the Display Book, or against an order held by a floor broker in the crowd, or from the specialist's own inventory. When all or part of an order has been filled, the system generates a report that goes to the investor who placed the order. Trades involving more than one SuperDOT order will produce more than one report.

The *Opening Automated Reporting System* (OARS) is a subsystem of SuperDOT. It focuses exclusively on the opening of the market. OARS will accept the premarket opening orders for all NYSE stocks up to 30,099 shares per order. OARS pairs up buy and sell orders continuously and automatically, and lets the specialist know if there are more sell than buy orders in any stock, or vice versa. OARS keeps performing these functions up until the market opens, thus helping the specialist figure out what the opening price for a stock will be.

NASDAQ.   Official Outlets: SOES and SelectNet. The Nasdaq's history of the way it treats the small investor has been spotty at best. In fact, numerous changes were made in 1997 after an extensive SEC investigation found that Nasdaq market makers were engaged in price-fixing, even going so far as blackballing and hounding with abusive phone calls any market maker who tried to give investors and traders better prices.

For nearly 10 years before that time, the only way small investors could gain electronic access to the Nasdaq system was through the *Small Order Execution System* (SOES). SOES itself was created out of a catastrophe. During the 1987 crash, individual investors couldn't reach their brokers or, even if they could, the brokers often were delayed in executing orders. There were even numerous instances where trading departments actually refused to take orders, let alone fill them.

In response to that disaster, the National Association of Securities Dealers, which administers Nasdaq, created SOES, a computerized system which requires that market makers execute orders of 1000 shares or less at the prices the Nasdaq market makers have posted. SOES is a system in which an individual launches the trade by responding to the market maker's advertised price for a given stock. An investor's SOES trades aren't negotiated. Instead, they're executed—instantly.

Those changes were revolutionary. Before SOES, market makers often would execute an order only if they felt it was to their advantage and they didn't have to buy or sell even at the prices they themselves had quoted. But, by 1998, the number of users was beginning to clog the SOES system and it continues to be clogged today. The result: execution is slow. And there is one more piece of frustration. Market makers are required to fill only 100 shares of a SOES order. If you want to trade more than 100 shares, then the rest of your order may go begging.

The advantages of SOES, the small-order system, engendered a demand for a similar system for market makers. The NASD responded in 1990 with SelectNet, the most immediate effect of which was to largely remove market making from the limitations of the telephone. Instead of having to call several—or more— colleagues to effect a trade, a task of many, perhaps crucial minutes, market makers now publish their intended trade on SelectNet. They instantly appears on the network's screens in every market maker's office. Because the system's computer mediates in every transaction, backing away from a trade, reneging, is no longer possible without penalty. In time, the NASD opened SelectNet to all traders.

In the now enlarged, hence more liquid, marketplace, traders can implement their trades via a *broadcast order*, which is entered to all market makers and is a totally voluntary system whereby the market maker is not obligated to execute, or a *preference order*, directed to a specific market maker. A *directed order* must be filled or killed within 10 seconds. During this gap between order and execution, the market, and prices, may move away. The market makers trade for their own accounts, and as such are competitors of other traders and will not execute orders that do not serve their own interests.

SelectNet has some interesting and profitable features. Traders' bids and offers, tendered only through market makers, do not appear on the Level II screen. By placing a SelectNet order, a trader can trade between the spread and perhaps win a better price. Or a market maker may need to buy a big block of stock and wish to do so secretly lest the purchase move the market. To implement the purchase, the market marker would be disposed to pay a price reasonably higher than the spread. A preference order could facilitate that.

In both SelectNet and SOES, the presence of the market maker between the trader and the implementation of the market marker's intentions forces the trader into reactivity; the trader reacts to the bids and offers the market maker establishes. Traders cannot freely and directly bid and ask; they cannot make their own market. Thus the impetus for the further transformation of trading: the advent of the ECN.

Electronic Communications Networks

Leveling the Playing Field. After the 1997 rule changes, *Electronic Communications Networks* (ECNs) materialized as a huge force in the trading world. Although some form of them had been around since the late 1960s, only big players such as banks or mutual funds could use them. Since 1997, anybody can, including traders. Now, they drive the Nasdaq market. Traders now favor the ECNs, even though they could use other systems. Why? The ECNs offer greater flexibility and faster executions, both critical aspects of any trader's strategy.

What are ECNs? Essentially, they are a third party. They are independent systems which have nothing to do with market makers, and that's to your advantage. What do they do? In essence, they are an electronic book of limit orders. If you have direct access to an ECN, then you may be able to see its entire limit book, although not all ECNs offer this advantage. When you can, you see what a specialist sees. Having access to the entire ECN limit book makes you a kind of specialist within that ECN.

There are several major advantages to ECNs. First, there is no human being arbitrarily saying yes, no, or maybe. Every bid, every offer, every execution is all done electronically.

This makes the trading process much more democratic. It's a lot easier to make trades because ECNs cut out the middlemen. There are no specialists or market makers to get in the way. You can buy or sell from anyone else using whatever ECN you're on. You might trade with a market maker, another trader, or mom and pop at home. ECNs don't care who or where you are, as long as you have the ability to make the trade. The result: you have a lot more outlets for buying and selling. There's no negotiating, no rules or apparatus dictating whether you'll be allowed to have an execution at a specific price.

ECNs also enable you to make your own market, to be active instead of passive. You can make your own bid and offer, just like the market makers. It's the difference between "selling to" and "selling through" an ECN. "Selling to" means that if an order is displayed on the bid/ask of a stock you want to buy or sell, you can buy or sell it. "Selling through" means you actually have access to the book. You can advertise your order, and that means you have a much greater likelihood of executing your deal, cutting the spread, and/or getting a better price. In short, if you don't like the deal the market maker is offering, you don't have to take it. You can try to make your own deal. Until ECNs were created, you had to take the market maker's deal on SOES or SelectNet or you had no deal at all.

Also, execution is almost instantaneous. The computer makes the matches among the deals; there are no humans involved, no market maker to slow down the process.

Four major ECNs dominate the field: Instinet, Island, REDI, and Archipelago. The most liquid are Instinet and Island, because they have the most people bidding for and offering stock. Most traders use them because it's a good idea to trade where a lot of other people are trading. Here are some details about each of the four ECNs:

1. Instinet is owned by Reuters, a British communications company. It's probably the biggest and most widely used of all the ECNs. Generally speaking, Instinet is where the institutions trade and where you'd want to trade if you were buying and selling in large blocks, say 5000 shares and up. Many traders prefer Instinet for any OTC trade of more than 1000 shares. Instinet also is well-known for its after-hours trading capacity.

2. Island was started in 1997 and is owned by Datek Online. It's now one of the most heavily used ECNs and accounts for approximately 10 percent of all Nasdaq trades. Island allows traders to broadcast their personal bids and offers to other traders around the world and to see the entire order book Island is offering.

3. REDI, owned by Spear, Leeds and Kellogg, the largest clearing firm on Wall Street, gives traders the capacity to place a market order on the Nasdaq, which no other system besides SOES does. At times, this feature can be very helpful. REDIBook also allows traders access to the NYSE.

4. Archipelago has several owners, including E*Trade, Goldman Sachs, Townsend Analytics, and Southwest Securities. It uses the SelectNet execution platform. A big advantage Archipelago has is that if it can't fill an order from its own book, it will open it up

to the national market. Archipelago has direct connections to Island, Instinet, and SelectNet. The company estimates that about one-third of its volume comes from traders or private customers using brokers or dealers.

Numerous other ECNs are available, and more are sure to come in the near future. Among them are Strike, ATTAIN, NEXTRADE, and Brut. Just remember that they each probably offer a feature or two which others don't. Which ones you'll use will depend on their liquidity and your personal trading system and preferences, as well as how much you value some features over others. You'll also want to consider cost in your personal equation.

Important Specifics to Remember for Various Routing Systems

1. **SOES.**   You can't place a SOES order from an ECN. SOES orders always go through a market maker. You cannot order through SOES if ECNs only (and no market makers) are on the inside market, which is the highest bid and lowest offer being offered between dealers. The dealers are offering the stock from their own inventory. Essentially, it's the wholesale market.

   SOES will also take market orders beginning as early as 7:30 A.M. Market orders placed before the market opens will be executed at the opening prices offered at 9:30 A.M. when the market opens. SOES will take orders of 100 to 1000 shares, and may fill any part of an order. Executions are first-come, first-served.

2. **SelectNet.**   Market makers can fill orders in any order they want, and can take any offer they want, regardless of who made the first offer. Your bid or offer is guaranteed for three minutes, although if it's outside the quote it might last longer. You can send your order to a specific market maker if you wish. This option is available only on SelectNet, which processes only limit orders.

   You can broadcast your bid or offer to all market makers or to a specific market maker, known as preference. Our recommendation: use preference. If you pick a particular market maker, they'll feel more obliged to execute your trade. All-or-none orders are accepted.

3. **Instinet.** Instinet is a separate market which may quote prices that are above or below the more traditional exchanges. You can trade both exchange-listed stocks and over-the-counter stocks from 6 A.M. to 7 P.M.

4. **SuperDOT.** Through SuperDOT, you can place both market and limit orders which will remain active for the remainder of the day they are placed. Orders are executed on a first-come, first-served basis. SuperDOT accepts market orders up to 30,999 shares and limit orders up to 99,999 shares.

5. **Island.** It processes only limit orders. The system can execute any part of an order.

   The drawback: Often Island doesn't fill the whole order, which is a big drawback of ECNs in general. Still, it's better to get part of your order executed than to have no deal at all.

NYSE Trading Versus NASDAQ Trading: Which Is for You?

1. The Nasdaq is quite volatile, which is excellent for traders, but only if they're highly experienced. Because this market is so volatile, it's unwise for you to trade more than two Nasdaq stocks at any given time. Greater volatility requires greater concentration, and because you can't use stops, you can't even go to the bathroom, or to lunch, or certainly on vacation, while you have a position in many Nasdaq stocks. Because of this volatility, prices can skyrocket higher or plunge a lot farther than they would on the NYSE.

2. New traders can be better off with the NYSE. You sometimes can get price improvement, better prices than you expected, on the NYSE. The stocks are very liquid. If you bid on a stock at $49^1/_2$, and a big block is sold at $49^1/_{16}$, your small trade may be included in the bigger one. This event might happen a few times a month, saving you some serious money.

   - The NYSE allows you to use stops. Nasdaq does not. Stops are essential to your strategy and your discipline. Before you buy any stock, you have to know at what price you will buy it, and at what price points above and below the purchase price you will sell. If you can use stops and you put them in place immediately after you buy a stock, you will be applying greater discipline than if you let your selling be swayed by emotion. You also will know your risk—how much you can lose on a trade. This gives us a strong defense as a foundation. Just as all championship sports teams start with a strong defense, so does a trading plan.

- You get tighter spreads. For example, on the Nasdaq, where prices are more volatile, the spread may be $91^1/_8$ to $91^3/_4$. You might put in a successful buy order at $91^1/_2$, but the price might suddenly plunge to 90. On the NYSE, if you bought at $91^3/_4$, likely the drop wouldn't be nearly as sharp or fast.

- You will know how big the inside market is. The NYSE specialist shows the true size and nature of the market 95 percent of the time. On the Nasdaq, a market maker may show 1000 shares available to sell when there are in fact 50,000.

- You can trade portfolio-style, so you can trade several stocks at the same time. Trading several stocks diversifies your investments and cuts your risk.

- On the NYSE, you eventually can trade big lots of very liquid stocks. On the Nasdaq, it's hard to trade more than 1000 shares at a time.

- Most of the NYSE stocks are very liquid. Many of the Nasdaq stocks have a limited demand, and so it's much harder to buy or sell them. The result: you might have to hang onto a stock a lot longer than you want to, resulting in larger losses than you expected.

3. Find the best style for you. Staring at a screen and tracking one or two stocks, the Nasdaq approach, is a very different feeling from tracking a whole portfolio of NYSE stocks. Ultimately, you've got to make the decision.

Brokers

The contest is between traditional brokers, on-line brokers and direct access brokers. Cost and execution speed are the variables you need to think about.

Traditional Brokers

The standard phone-based brokers simply aren't suitable for trading. They aren't in a position to execute your orders as fast as a trader wants and needs. Why? You must call the broker, give the order, wait for the order to be filled, then get confirmation. In the world of trading, that can take several minutes or more, a very long time for traders.

If you do use a standard broker, remember to find one who works on an agency, not a principal, basis. The principal-basis brokers are simply order-takers. You call them, give them the order, then they fill it precisely as you describe it.

Agency-based brokers will try to find you a better deal by using several different order systems. They might shave $1/8$, $1/2$, or even a full point off what you ordered and pass the savings along to you. In short, they're on your side, working for you. If the principal-based broker got a better deal, you wouldn't see it. The brokerage would buy it at the cheaper price or sell it at a higher price for its own account, then pass the results to you at precisely the price you ordered, pocketing the extra profit.

Typically, phone-based brokers have higher commissions than on-line or direct access brokers. An agency firm might charge a $35 commission, but these firms say they also get you a better deal by improving your execution price.

On-Line Brokers

These brokers basically utilize the Internet as their front end. Often, trading through an on-line broker is far less expensive than dealing with a phone-based broker, and you get faster execution. On-line brokers are good if you trade only a few times a month, but they're not geared to serious trading.

On-line brokers have several drawbacks:

- Often, on-line brokers are just middlemen in the process and don't execute the trades themselves. They won't have the ability to execute the order. They use the Internet to send your order to brokers and dealers who can execute it, and you can end up paying extra for them to do it. (See "Payment for Order Flow" following).

- The order might be delayed or might not be filled at all because you haven't received an execution report while the on-line broker is sending your order to someone else to actually do the trade. You can't sell your stock until you have an execution report. Time is money.

- On-line brokers have the same trouble as you and I do reaching the order desk where the trade is actually made. That problem crops up particularly during high-volume or fast-moving markets.

- In a fast-moving market, the prices displayed by an on-line broker may lag behind where the market actually is. The result: you might pay too much for a stock or make a wrong decision.

Direct Access Brokers

Direct access brokers have the best execution because they don't farm out their order execution and you don't pay for someone else to execute the trade. They don't work through the Internet. They have a direct pipeline to NYSE specialists, Nasdaq market makers, as well as ECNs, SOES, and SelectNet. You control the execution because your order isn't farmed out. That's because you have direct access to the people who take your execution orders. The direct access brokers have higher commissions, but they can actually be less expensive than the on-line brokers because you're not paying for order flow.

Payment for Order Flow.   With direct access brokers, you won't end up paying a "rebate" for using a particular Nasdaq market maker to execute your order. Payment for order flow is one of the industry's dirty little secrets. Essentially, a brokerage firm routes orders to certain market makers, who then rebate 1 to 4 cents a share to the brokerage for the order. These payments are the life blood of discount brokers, who can charge penny-ante commissions because they get these rebates. In addition, a brokerage house can even fill an order from its own internal order desk—yes, it's legal—but you may not get the best price.

So widespread and tainted has payment for order flow become that Securities and Exchange Commission Chairman Arthur Levitt recently gave a speech in which he said, "When a broker-deal sells the customer order flow to a designated market maker or exchange, the question of whose interest is being served—the broker's or the customer's—is squarely raised," he said.

Tools

The biggest tool you'll have at your disposal when you trade on the Nasdaq system is having Level II quotes. There are three Nasdaq levels of quotes you could theoretically have on your computer screen:

Level I.   This level is the most basic. It offers the inside market only. The inside market is the same quote brokers usually give. It looks like this: Microsoft 56 bid, 56^1/$_8$ offer.

Level II.   This level is essential for short-term traders. It's used for Nasdaq trading, day trading, and any short-term trade that could turn into a day trade. Level II used to be available only to NASD members or registered market makers. This level, when you're trading on the Nasdaq, is the trader's most powerful tool. Why? Because it shows all the market makers and ECNs along with their quotes and size. That's powerful. You can trade directly with the market makers and other traders, bypassing all the middlemen. The system is fast, accurate, and gives you complete control. The longer your trading time frame, the less you need it; however, you can't day trade without it. Figure 2-5 shows what a Level II quote looks like.

Level III.   These quotation systems are reserved for the market makers. Appearing almost identical to a Nasdaq Level II system, Level III also allows a trader to create bids and offers on the national market.

Important Indices.   There are several indices you need to know about. They are:

■ **The Dow Jones Average.**   This index is based on the prices of a specific number of stocks drawn from four separate categories: (1) The Utilities Average, 15 stocks, (2) The Transportation Average, 20 stocks, (3) The Industrial Average, 30 stocks, and (4) The Composite Average (all 65 stocks from the other three averages).

XYZ Corp.						
last	101¹/₁₆	bid	101¹/₁₆	high	101³/₁₆
open	99¹/₂	ask	101¹/₈	low	101¹/₁₆
close	99¹/₄	size	20 x 10	volume	1438700
change	+¹³/₁₆				

JPMS	101¹/₁₆	20	REDI	101¹/₈	5
INCA	101¹/₁₆	5	DKNY	101¹/₈	10
ISLD	101¹/₁₆	3	SHWD	101¹/₈	5
GSCO	101¹/₁₆	10	FBCO	101¹/₈	5
PWJC	101	5	ISLD	101¹/₄	6
PRUS	101	10	MONT	101¹/₄	10
ARCA	100¹⁵/₁₆	2	ARCA	101¹/₄	5
BRUT	100¹⁵/₁₆	8	MWSE	101⁵/₁₆	1
RSSF	100¹⁵/₁₆	10	PRUS	101⁵/₁₆	1
			GSCO	101⁵/₁₆	1
SBSH	101¹/₁₆	1	LFHM	101⁵/₁₆	1

Figure 2-5. A Level II quote.

- **Standard & Poor's 500.** Also known as the S&P 500, it's based on the stock prices of 40 public utilities, 40 financial stocks, 20 transportation stocks, and 400 industrials. Each stock is value-weighted, that is, weighted according to the total value of its outstanding shares.

- **The S&P 100 Index.** This index value-weighs 100 blue-chip stocks, including such stalwarts as General Motors, Xerox, and IBM.

- **The NYSE Index.** This index value-weighs all the common stocks listed on the exchange.

- **The Wilshire 5000 Equity Index.** This index is by far the most comprehensive and broadest measure of the entire market. It value-weighs 5000 stocks from the NYSE, the American Stock Exchange, and the OTC market.

Short Selling

This maneuver essentially means you're betting that the price of a stock you have borrowed will go down. Be aware that theoretically your losses on a short sale could go to infinity. You could lose your entire account and all of your assets.

A short sale means you sell stock you don't own in hopes of making a profit on stock you will buy later. Here's how a short sale works:

1. First, you call your broker and ask if you can borrow the number of shares you want of the stock you want.
2. The broker will tell you whether that amount of that stock can be borrowed.
3. Those shares are reserved in your name for that day only, should you decide to execute the short sale.

Short Sale Rule.   When you do execute your short sale, you are required to do it on an *uptick*, when the price has moved up from the previous price for that stock, or on a *zero uptick*, when the price for a stock is the same as the previous sale following an uptick. For example:

50 to $50^1/_{16}$—short sale OK

50 to $49^1/_2$—short sale barred

50 to $49^1/_2$ to $48^5/_{16}$—short sale barred

50 to $49^1/_2$ to $48^5/_{16}$ to 49—short sale OK on last price

50 to $49^7/_8$ to 50 to 50—short sale OK on last two prices

News

You must keep up with what is going on in the financial world, as well as stocks you care about in particular, and the world in general. You should stay abreast of what *Barron's*, CNN, the *Wall Street Journal*, the *Investor's Business Daily*, and the *New York Times* have to say. Information is a trader's primary source of ideas. Without it, the heart of your strategy stops working. If you don't know what the news is, you don't have information crucial to your trading decisions. News and trading strategies based on the news will be covered in later chapters.

Trading Basics
Review Questions

1. The price a trader broadcasts to sell stock.
   a. Bid
   b. Market
   c. Ask
   d. Closing price

2. The price a trader broadcasts to buy stock.
   a. At market
   b. Bid
   c. Ask
   d. Closing price

3. The term most often used to describe a large transaction (10,000 shares or more) of a particular stock.
   a. Tier
   b. Gross
   c. Unit
   d. Block

4. If you give an instruction to buy or sell stock at "best price," this would be equivalent to
   a. at market.
   b. at the money.
   c. bid.
   d. closing price.

5. Nasdaq Level II displays the
   a. inside market of all market makers in Nasdaq stocks, including quote size.
   b. inside market of all market makers in Nasdaq stocks, excluding quote size.
   c. complete quotes of all market makers in Nasdaq stocks, including quote size.
   d. complete quotes of all market makers in Nasdaq stocks, excluding quote size.

6. Which of the following are true? NYSE Super Dot System
    1. has no order size limit.
    2. orders are placed on the specialist's book.
    3. market orders are not accepted.
    4. execution reports are routed directly to broker/dealer via computer.
        a. 1 only
        b. 1 and 3
        c. 2 and 4
        d. all of the above

7. Sell stop orders can be used to
    1. limit loss on short positions.
    2. limit loss on long positions.
    3. sell stock if a support level is broken.
    4. sell stock if a resistance level is broken.
        a. 1 and 2
        b. 2 and 4
        c. 1 and 4
        d. 2 and 3

8. SOES . . .
    1. is an automated trading system.
    2. handles only NYSE stocks.
    3. handles trades of no more than 1000 shares.
    4. is exempt from the uptick rule.
        a. 1 and 2
        b. 1 and 3
        c. 2, 3, and 4
        d. all of the above

9. To protect a gain on a long stock position a trader should use a
    a. buy stop order.
    b. sell stop order.
    c. sell limit order.
    d. immediate or cancel order.

10. Direct trading between institutions OTC is an example of a _____ market trade.

    a. first

    b. second

    c. third

    d. fourth

11. Buy 1000 shares ABC 70 limit GTC. If ABC trades at a high of 77 and a low of 74 for the day, this order

    a. has been filled.

    b. was not filled.

    c. must be resubmitted.

    d. was cancelled.

Define. Choose a corresponding letter which can be used only once.

12. Resistance

13. Trend

14. Short covering

15. Volume

16. Over-the-counter market

17. Market value

18. Fill

    a. Decentralized, negotiated market in which dealers execute trades over an electronic trading system.

    b. An order is executed.

    c. The closing of a short stock position by purchasing the shares in the market and using these to replace the shares that were borrowed.

    d. A price level to which a stock rises (and then falls from) repeatedly.

    e. The up, down, or sideways movement of a stock over a period of time.

    f. The total number of shares traded in a given period of time.

    g. The price of a security.

Trading Basics
Review Answers

1. C
2. B
3. D
4. A
5. C
6. C
7. D
8. B
9. B
10. D
11. B
12. D
13. E
14. C
15. F
16. A
17. G
18. B

3

THE WHAT AND WHEN OF TECHNICAL ANALYSIS

Introduction to Analysis

THE LEADING METHODS OF PEERING into the future of stocks and markets and of reaching a trading decision are fundamental and technical analysis. The distinction between them blurs, but some differences remain clear. *Fundamental analysis* addresses factors of supply and demand. Analysts look for it in the entrails of annual reports and other compilations of numbers. Demand for stock in, say, a coffee company is partly a function of earnings, confidence in the economy, and what the Federal Reserve Bank is likely to do with interest rates. The supply of coffee, on the other hand, is a function of, among other factors, weather and political conditions in the growing region. After evaluating many of the identifiable factors, the fundamentalist tries to predict the price of coffee. Technical analysts, or technicians, evaluate market and market-related data in order to form buy and sell decisions. Analysts massage their data to highlight market trends, moving averages, oscillators, and other indicators. Other technicians plot charts of those data and look for patterns, just as the ancients sought constellations among the random stars. Terms such as market, trends, momentum, and up-and-down ticks describe the aggregate behavior of individuals who are buying and selling securities. Chartists, who go to the extremes in abstraction, are mapping aggregate human behavior. They look for head-and-shoulder, wedge, and other formations; for single, double, and triple tops and bottoms; and for breakouts and breakdowns. And they bring to their search computer artificial intelligence and pattern-recognition programs. Thus, technicians, and especially chartists, try to discover from historical patterns when similar patterns may occur, and relate these to buying and selling decisions. Their methods rest in large part on the assumption that history repeats itself and that many of history's details repeat themselves. To the extent they do not, technicians fill the gaps with intuition and preference. And despite the precision implied by graph paper, and curves and lines, technical analysis is not a science, which demands absolute predictability, but a useful art. And ultimately, the efforts of both technical and fundamental analysts leave appreciable residues of uncertainty, and that is what Wall Street deals in. The consensus is represented in the price of a security: the greater the residue (decreased visibility) the lower the price, generally, and the greater the possible reward; and vice versa.

What, exactly, is technical analysis? Remember when your high school history teacher told you that understanding the past would tell you a lot about what would happen in the future? Well, that's what technical analysis is about. In terms of trading, you could look at it as both technical and fundamental analysts use history when trying to predict a stock's movement, and your Level II screen on your computer uses the present. You need data from both the past and present.

Technical analysis studies how the price of a stock has acted in the past in order to predict how it's going to act in the future. The primary tool involved is the chart, plus some mathematical indicators, which you use to identify trends. Trends are patterns, ways in which the price of a stock has acted before. Technical analysts believe that knowing what each stock's trends are will point you toward the direction in which you should be making your trades. Technical analysts examine market-related data so they can decide when to buy and sell. The most common data are the market's open, high, low, close, and volume.

In this chapter you'll be taking a look at two parts of technical analysis. The first part will cover what technical analysis is and how to gather the information. The second part will examine how to apply the information you've gathered.

The support for technical analysis rests on several beliefs:

1. The price of a stock is the consensus of all the people interested in that stock as to what its price ought to be.

2. Price is everything. Technical analysts believe that the price is the prime barometer for all the factors which could affect a stock. However, some other indicators may be necessary.

3. Prices move up, down, and even sideways, in patterns. Those patterns are the keys to technical analysis.

4. A stock's price history patterns will repeat themselves. The patterns you discover worked before, so they likely will work again.

5. Because human beings are involved in a stock's pricing, technical analysis offers you probabilities, not certainties. No matter how good your analysis, nothing in the stock market is surefire because human emotions come into play. Technical analysis is ultimately a useful art. It will never be a science. Even the best chart readers might disagree on the nature of a specific chart.

6. Before a significant price change will happen, the price will trade in a sideways range. After all the institutional investors have bought (accumulated) or sold (distributed) as much stock as they want, there aren't a lot of shares available. At that point, the stock may be poised for a sustained move. Accumulation,

or buying of shares, may be a sign of a sustained move up; distribution, or selling of shares, may be a sign of a sustained move down.

7. The longer one of those accumulation or distribution periods is, the larger the expected move—up or down—will be.

8. Each stock has its own personality. Compare Coke and Juniper Networks, for example. Each stock's volatility and range are quite different compared to the other. Volatility is how much a stock's price goes up and down and how often. Coke is a fairly stable and predictable stock which may go up or down perhaps three to four points in a week. Many Nasdaq technology high-flyers could rise or fall 10 or more points in a given day. Coke's range recently was a high of 64 to a low of 43 for a 12-month period. Juniper Networks' was a high of 245 and a low of 23.

9. As a technical analyst, you don't have to rely heavily on charts, but almost every technical analyst does. They consider charts to be their absolute best tool, and you may, too.

10. It is almost always suitable to buy at support or sell at resistance, regardless of the fundamentals.

So, what good will technical analysis do for you and your trading strategy? It will show you the best stocks to trade, as well as when to buy and sell them. It gives you an edge. It gives you information which, if your analysis is right, allows you to buy on a rising price trend and sell on a falling price trend.

With technical analysis, you start with six basic questions:

1. At what prices has the stock been recently?

2. Is a trend just beginning or about to peak out? If it's at the top of a chart, then the trend may be ending. If it's at the bottom, then the trend may be just beginning.

3. What's the stock's range?

4. How does the stock typically trade over a given period of time, whether it's a day, two days, three days, or whatever your standard holding period is?

5. After looking over Question 4, ask yourself, "Is the stock too volatile for my trading strategy?"

6. Where is the stock going in the next several days?

Basic Tools

If you're going to use price charts of a stock, you're going to need to analyze some basic pieces of information: *time, price,* and *volume.* Those three factors are what price charts show (see Figure 3-1). The information you should have at hand includes two kinds of specific stock information:

First is the high, low, and range. The high is the most that was paid for the stock over a specific period of *time,* whether it's two hours or 60 days, while the low is the least anyone paid for that stock during the same period of time. The range shows both the high and low. For example, if the high is 85, and the low is 50, the range would be 50 to 85.

Second is the open and close. The open is the *price* of a share of stock at the start of any given trading period, and the close is the price of that same share of stock at the end of that trading period.

Then there's a piece of market information you'll need: volume. Volume is the total number of shares traded in a specific market during a specific time period, whether it's a day—which is the most common measure—or a month, or whatever time period you choose.

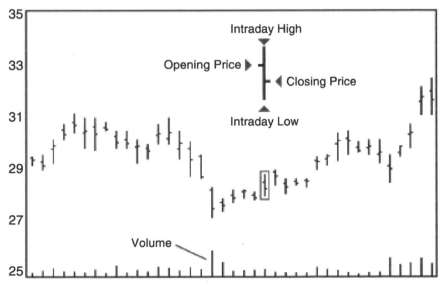

Figure 3-1. A price chart showing time, price, and volume.

Charts: What You Need to Know

Charts will tell you a lot about any given stock, but just remember that there is no ultimate truth in charts. The best people in the field might read the same chart differently, so don't look to mighty gurus for some kind of divine guidance. You'll have to learn and interpret on your own. It's your money, after all. You've got to take the responsibility for your decisions.

What do charts tell you? No matter what kind you use, price charts give you the same information: where prices have been, what the market trends are, important previous low and high prices, and a general idea of how volatile the market is. That kind of information suggests what your best trading strategies might be and which markets would be best for your trading.

Trends

You'll need to know a lot about trends in order to understand technical analysis. First, what is a *trend*? It's a time measurement of what directions price levels are heading. No market or stock moves in a straight line; they rise and fall in a general direction. There are times when the market or stock will even move sideways. There will be pauses in a trend, and trends will reverse; of course, it's important to be able to tell the difference between the two.

You can read many trends into the same set of information, but there are three that technical analysts use the most:

1. **The primary trend,** also known as the major or long-term trend. It lasts between six months to several years but usually lasts from one to two years. In effect, it's a consensus of how investors feel about business in general. When charted, a business cycle appears as a rounded peak between two troughs which are three to fours years apart. The primary trend—bullish or bearish—lasts for a year or two, but not symmetrically. Bull markets generally last longer.

   Three phases characterize a major or primary trend: accumulation, markup, and distribution. During the accumulation phase, only traders who have spotted the earliest signs of the trend are buying the stock. Everybody else is staying away. Then the markup phase hits. That's when a lot more people start noticing the stock and more people start buying it. In the distribution phase, the stock has reached a point where it's fairly valued, or maybe it's even overvalued. At this point, the smart traders have recognized this and bail out by selling, or distributing, their holdings.

2. **Secondary or intermediate trends.**   These trends move back and forth within the primary trend, and last from one to six months. They are considered corrections to the primary trend. It's important to know the direction and length of a primary trend, but you also can use intermediate trends to refine your trading strategies and to assess when the primary movement may have run its course.

3. **Minor or short-term trends.**   These trends are correction phases and are of special interest to traders rather than investors. Just as intermediate trends appear as rises and falls within a major trend, so do short-term trends appear as rises and falls within an intermediate trend. The hard part is identifying them. Longer-term trends are much easier to identify than intermediate ones, and short-term trends are the hardest of all to spot. These rises and falls are called *oscillations*, and are used to measure the velocity, or momentum, of price movements.

So, how do you chart the ups and downs of a stock or a market? With trendlines. *Trendlines* have a very precise definition: They are a sloping straight line which connects three or more lows in an uptrend or three or more highs in a downtrend. Generally, a market going up won't suddenly start going down and a market heading down won't suddenly start heading up.

Incidentally, when a market does break its trendline, that development could show that the trend itself is accelerating, and the market might continue in the same direction it's heading.

In reading charts, there are a few characteristics you'll be looking for, some of which have to do with specific prices, and some of which have to do with areas on the chart. First, the specific price indicators: the downtrend and the uptrend.

In the downtrend, the market for the stock in this situation is going down, but not usually in a straight line. It will go down, then come back up somewhat, then go down again, then up somewhat, then down again. Each peak on the chart is lower than the last peak, and each trough is lower than the last trough. Downtrend lines are shown by trendlines between three or more high points to show price resistance. When drawing downtrend lines, attach highs to each other in a straight line by drawing your chart lines from left to right (see Figure 3-2).

In an uptrend chart, you'll see the market for a specific stock going up and falling back, going up and falling back. The clue that it's an uptrend is that each peak, or top, is higher than the last peak, and each trough, or downturn, is higher than the last one, too. In Figure 3-3, notice how the line drawn between two or more troughs is rising. That's an uptrend line, and it shows price support. Take a look at Figure 3-3 as a classic example of a market in an uptrend.

Now, take a look at the two pieces of information on a stock chart which aren't very precise: support levels and resistance levels. They're an area on a chart, not a specific price point. A support level is the point where you expect the price to stop dropping because a lot of people will be buying the stock at that price. If a stock generally trades between 40 and 60, then 40 would be its support level (see Figure 3-4).

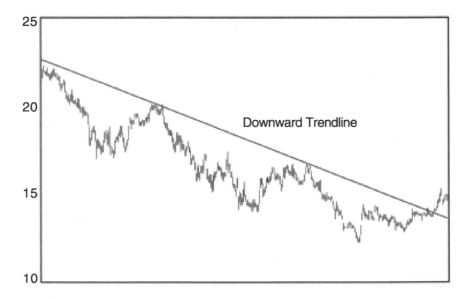

Figure 3-2.   Downtrend chart.

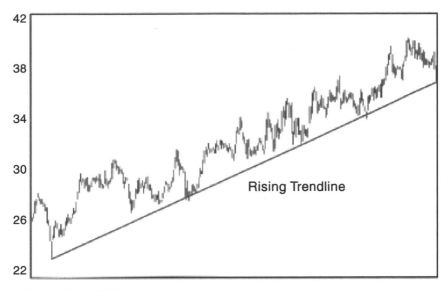

Figure 3-3. Uptrend chart.

If the price of a stock drops through its support level, that's a sign that the stock could be in deep trouble. Good for short sellers, perhaps, but bad news for everyone else.

The other area, as opposed to a specific price point, is the resistance level. It's an area on the chart which is above the present price. When you identify a resistance point, you're anticipating that a lot of people will be selling the stock then, cutting short the rise in the stock's price. This area is often the result of some previous highs having been reached in that same area. If a stock is trading between 40 and 60, 60 would be the resistance level (see Figure 3-5). Note that once a stock's price bursts through its support level, that support level can become a resistance level. For example, let's say that the stock selling between 40 and 60 breaks through the $60 mark and now is selling for $64 a share. That $60 price could now become a new support level. If the stock price now falls below that $60 mark, the price could be in trouble. The $60 mark, which had been a high point (a resistance level), has now become a low point (support level).

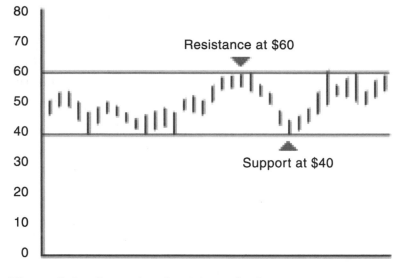

Figure 3-4. Support and resistance levels.

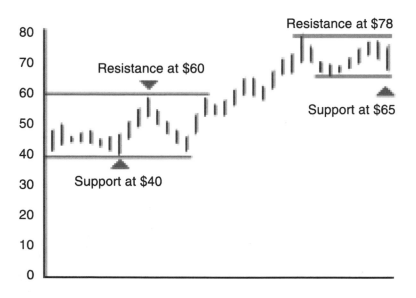

Figure 3-5. Support level can become a resistance level.

Of course, a support level could become a resistance level. If that stock trading between 40 and 60 should drop below the 40 level, then 40 could become a new resistance level (see Figure 3-6). That would mean that the price of the stock would have trouble rising through the 40 level to climb back to its former heights. The $40 price, which had been a low point (support level), has now become a high point (resistance level).

Another technical analysis piece of information you'll want to track is volume. A stock's volume should expand when the stock price is going up and shrink when it's going down. When the volume doesn't follow that pattern, that may be an early sign that the stock's price will be heading in the other direction in the near future (see Figure 3-7).

For example, suppose the volume has been acting normally, with higher volume as the price climbs and lower volume when it falls back. Then, suddenly, volume shrinks when the price goes up and expands when the price goes down. Those signals say that the price might be dropping shortly, and you should be attuned to that possibility. Generally, when a stock price reaches a breakout point—which is when it crashes through a resistance level—you should see increased volume. If a price hits a new low but the volume doesn't,

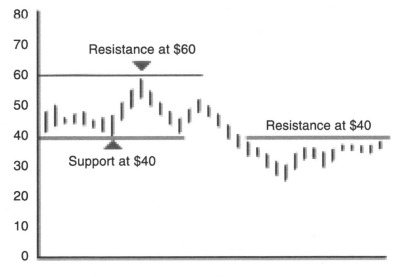

Figure 3-6. A new resistance level.

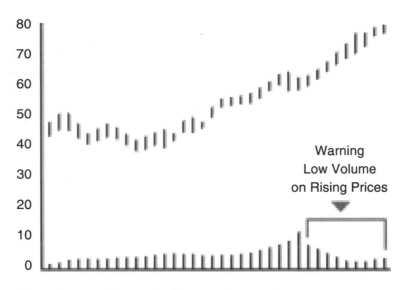

Figure 3-7. Volume should expand as stock price rises.

that could be a buy signal. Here's a general guideline: watch for big jumps in the volume. One good measure is if the volume in one day is three times the average volume for the previous five days, that's a sign that a big buyer is interested and you may want to jump on the train. This rule of thumb works best when the volume increases when there's no news. That means people "in the know" are buying in anticipation of news.

Patterns

Charts actually can fall into patterns that form highly significant shapes. There are many such patterns, some with very exotic names. Here are a few of the most important, which you should work to recognize:

1. **Head-and-shoulders.**   This pattern is one of the best known and most reliable, but, like all other pieces of technical analysis, it's not foolproof. It looks like a head with a shoulder on each side. This pattern shows an uptrend when both the highs and lows for a stock keep going higher. If a stock has a high of 49, 53, and 59,

and the lows are $46^{1}/_{8}$, $47^{5}/_{8}$ and $51^{1}/_{2}$, both the highs and lows are rising. In a typical situation, the "left shoulder" and the "head" are the last two highs which show an increase. The "right shoulder" materializes when the price falls, then pushes somewhat higher, only to fall back through the "neckline." At that point the lows of the left shoulder and the head are connected (see Figure 3-8). This patterns shows that an uptrend is ending. Note: An upside-down head-and-shoulders often materializes when a market is bottoming.

2. **Rounding tops and bottoms.** The rounding top happens when sentiment gradually shifts from bullish to bearish. Rounding bottoms happen when expectations gradually move from bearish to bullish, as shown in Figure 3-9.

3. **Double tops and bottoms.** A double top occurs when prices move to a resistance level on significant volume, then fall back, then return to the resistance level but with smaller volume. At that point, prices then start to drop, signifying a new downtrend. A double bottom has the same qualities as a double top, but it's upside-down (see Figure 3-10).

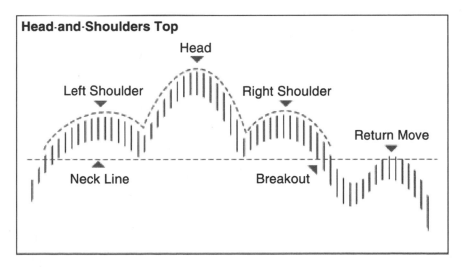

Figure 3-8. Head-and-shoulders pattern.

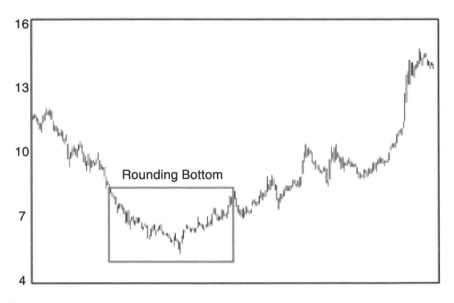

Figure 3-9. Rounding bottom pattern.

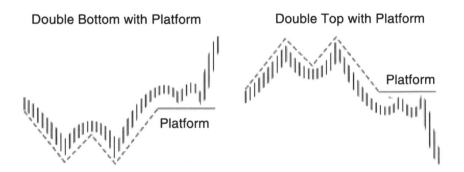

Figure 3-10. Double tops and bottoms pattern.

4. **Gaps.** In charts, gaps are highly significant because they show strong demand. They show themselves as breaks in the graph where a stock opens significantly higher than the high of the previous day and preserves that higher price throughout that day. There are three kinds of gaps:

- **The breakaway.** Occurs when a stock gaps out of a trading range. Breakaway gaps (see Figure 3-11) usually signal the beginning of an up or down price move and they're the best kind of gap for a trader.
- **The continuation.** In this gap, the price of the stock already has been rising. After the gap occurs, the stock's price continues to climb. A continuation gap usually happens about halfway in a stock's rise (see Figure 3-12).
- **The exhaustion.** This gap materializes at the end of the upward cycle (see Figure 3-13). You can spot it because it is accompanied by volume which is massive for that particular stock. It's a final push toward new highs. The activity here is a good time to bail out while there are still buyers.

One common kind of pattern in exhaustion gaps is the *island reversal,* in which a stock trades in a range which may only be a couple of points for a couple of days. At that point, last-minute buyers or sellers might reverse their position, selling if they've been buying, or buying if they've been selling. This activity creates a gap in the opposite direction. The shape of the gap looks like an island surrounded by water and usually signals that a trend is about to reverse—strongly (see Figure 3-14).

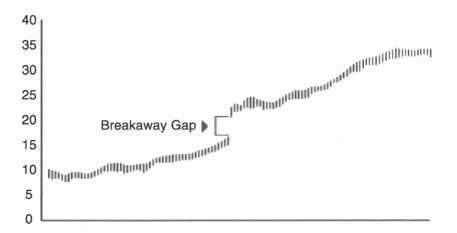

Figure 3-11. Breakaway gaps are the best kind for traders.

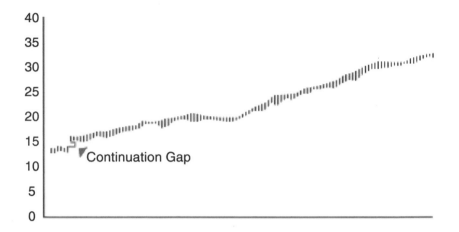

Figure 3-12. After a continuation gap, a stock's price continues to climb.

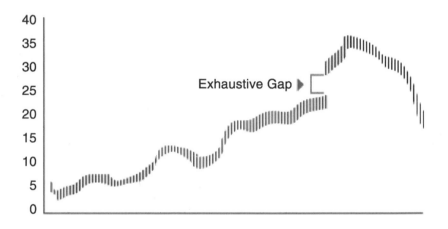

Figure 3-13. The exhaustion gap is a final push toward new highs.

There are a few cautions on gaps. First, avoid stocks which don't have much liquidity; it's too easy for traders to cause a gap. Second, don't jump on gaps caused because brokers are recommending the stock. They could change their minds all too easily.

However, if gaps result from something more substantial, such as higher earnings or corporate announcements, then the gaps are much more solid. If the gaps have broken out of a trading range as well, that's a very good sign.

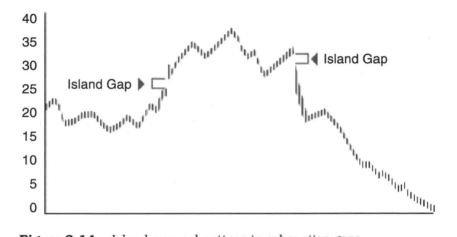

Figure 3-14.   Island reversal pattern in exhaustion gaps.

There are two situations which are particularly strong candidates for gap follow-through. Watch the stocks which have a relatively small float, say, 10 to 20 million. Also, watch for stocks which have a truly strong earnings surge, usually an average of 100 percent earnings rise during each of the last two quarters; then you should be watching for gaps in this stock very, very closely.

Kinds Of Charts

There are two kinds of charts you should know about. First is the *bar chart*. The most popular kind of chart, this graph sums up a stock's price highs and lows and its open and close over a given time span. A vertical line shows the highs and lows of the price for any given time period. Look at the bar's top to see the high, look at the bottom to see the low (see Figure 3-15). The opens and closes are shown by lines perpendicular to the line showing the highs and lows. The closing price is indicated with a perpendicular line meeting the vertical line on the right; the opening price is shown by a perpendicular line meeting the vertical line on the left. You can use bar charts to show any number of time frames, whether you want a minute or a month, a week or a year.

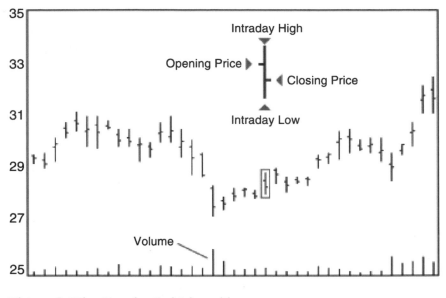

Figure 3-15. Bar chart's high and low.

The second kind of chart is the candlestick chart (see Figure 3-16). Originated in Japan, these charts are like bar charts, but instead of bars they use rectangles showing the opening and closing prices for a particular trading day, week, month, or any time frame you want.

Part of reading candlestick charts really is a matter of black and white. If the rectangle is black, the closing price is lower than the opening price. If it's white, the closing price was higher than the opening price.

The candles even have small shapes resembling wicks, which are above and below the rectangles (see Figure 3-17). The wick above the candle shows the highest price in that particular time period, and the wick below the candle shows the lowest price. The candlestick charts are useful because they visually show a stock's close in relation to its open in a way that the bar chart does not. A short-term trader needs to be aware of this relationship. Some technical analysts also believe candlesticks show specific price patterns not shown on bar charts.

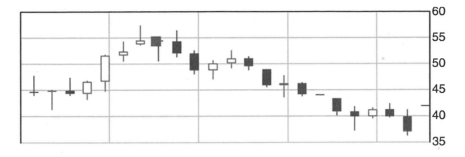

Figure 3-16. Candlestick chart.

Candlestick Charts

◀ Highest Price

◀ Opening Price

Filled indicates closing price is lower than the opening price

◀ Closing Price

◀ Lowest Price

___

◀ Highest Price

◀ Opening Price

Hollow indicates opening price is greater than the closing price

◀ Closing Price

◀ Lowest Price

Figure 3-17. Reading candlestick charts.

There are hundreds of different candlestick lines and patterns. In fact, entire books have been written about the subject. Don't worry about becoming technical to that degree. At this point, just be aware that candlesticks are a form of chart you may want to know about.

CAUTION: *Traders are tempted to add one technical analysis study after another. If a trade goes bad, they continue to filter their system until they find a winning method. This is not effective. Anomalies to your technical analysis are not good. Technical analysis is a tool, not a toy, and it's not meant to prove that you were right. Remember one of the "Trading Basics" chapter's don'ts: Don't have a need to be right. If the trade goes bad, admit it, sell it, and move on. The best technical analysis studies are generally the simplest.*

Go or No-Go: Deciding When to Get in and When to Get Out

Now you know something about how to make charts and analyze stocks from a technical perspective. All that knowledge will help you gather the information you need. Still, you have to decide when to buy a stock and when to sell it. Timing is crucial in any short-term trade. Your profits and losses can be larger or smaller, depending on when you get in and get out. Even if you're right about the market trends, you could lose money consistently if you didn't get in and get out at the right times. The following information is a bundle of tools which will help you make those decisions.

Indicators

Indicators are formulas which use raw market data such as the high, low, close, and volume in a very specific way. The results are plotted on a chart. They sometimes produce patterns which will help you in formulating your strategy.

Moving Average. One of the most useful and most frequently used indicators, the moving average is the average price for a stock over a given period of time, whether it is for a couple of days or a couple of years, showing trends (see Figure 3-18). The moving average is the average price of a security at any given time. You would get the moving average of a stock for the last 30 days if you added

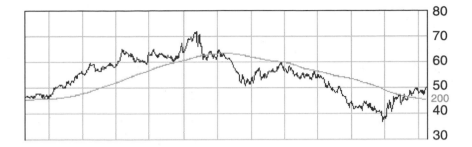

Figure 3-18. Moving average indicator.

the closing prices for the most recent 30 days and then divided by 30. The shorter the time period, such as the last two or three days, the closer the moving average will be to the stock's actual price. The most common time periods are 5, 10, 20, 40, 50, and 200 days.

Here is an easy way to evaluate a stock's moving average. If the stock is trading above its 200-day moving average, then you've spotted an uptrend, and if the stock is trading below the 200-day mark, it's a downtrend. If a stock's price gaps below its 200-day average, that's a very strong sell signal. If a stock is 50 percent or more above its 200-day moving average, that's a good time to sell, too.

The moving average is useful for spotting market trends, too. If the majority of stocks are trading above their 200-day average, it's an uptrend; below the 200-day average, it's a downtrend.

Here are two quick moving average review tips. First, stocks trading above their 200-day moving average for some time are in an uptrend, and those trading below that mark are in a downtrend.

Second, be aware of extremes. A stock trading way above or below its 200-day moving average might be headed for a correction. And a stock that has a break, or sudden marked drop, below its 200-day moving average line could be poised to head even lower.

Remember, moving averages won't get you into a stock when the price hits bottom, and they won't get you out when a stock is selling at its peak price. However, moving averages will help you catch major trends, and that alone makes it a very useful and quite common tool. Many institutions buy and sell around major averages.

Relative Strength

A very important concept, relative strength compares how strong the stock you're analyzing is to a group of stocks or the entire broader market. It examines how well the stock rises in a rising market and how much a stock falls in a falling market. A stock which gains momentum when the market is advancing, or doesn't lose a lot of its value when the market is declining, is a stock worth considering. A strong stock in a weak market is a good buy candidate. If a stock is weak in a strong market, that stock would be a good prospect for a short sale when the market starts going downhill.

This gauge is good for both the industry group in which your stock is located and for the broader market as a whole. This strategy is particularly useful when carrying positions overnight, and deciding whether you think a stock will be a strong or weak performer when the market opens the next day.

The way to gauge the strength or weakness of a stock is to compare it to an index or set of indices you think form the best basis of comparison. That means you'll use indices to track the health of various sectors of the market. Whatever kind of index you're looking for, you'll find it. There are a few you should know about.

Indices

The Dow Jones Industrial Average.   This average covers only 30 stocks. Although a lot of professionals prefer a broader cross-section of the market than the DJIA offers, it's still a useful gauge of how the market is doing (see Figure 3-19).

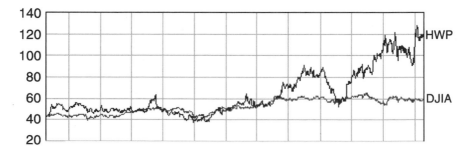

Figure 3-19. Dow Jones Industrial Average index.

Standard & Poor's 500 Composite Index.   This index has more than 10 times the number of companies than the DJIA, so professionals value it more as a gauge of the broader market. It tracks stocks in four sectors: financial, industrial, transportation, and utility. All of the companies are large capitalization stocks, meaning their outstanding shares are usually worth at least $5 billion. In addition, the index weights the companies by how many outstanding shares they have (see Figure 3-20). That means a $1 change in Microsoft would have a lot more impact than a $1 change in Florida Power & Light or the supermarket chain Winn-Dixie, because Microsoft has so many more shares in the market than the other two.

Russell 3000.   This index measures how well or how poorly 3000 of the largest capitalization companies in the United States are doing. It covers about 98 percent of all stocks on the market.

Wilshire 5000.   One of the most widely watched indices for gauging the health of the broad market, this index actually covers 7000 U.S. companies. Each stock in the index is weighted by how large or small its capitalization is.

There are many more indices, and if you want one that tracks a highly specialized sector containing the stocks you like the most, it's out there. Some of these are the S&P 100 Index, Healthcare Index, Midcap 400 Sector Indices, Midcap 400 Total Return, Nasdaq Biotech Index, Computer Index, Financial Index, Nasdaq-100, OTC Index-Composite, OTC Index-Banking, and OTC Index-Industrials.

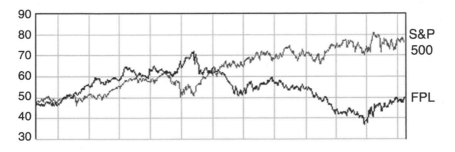

Figure 3-20.   S&P 100 index.

If you find a stock which is strong when its index is weak, then you've found a strong buy candidate when the market roars back. You can use relative strength for time periods as short as an hour and as long as weeks or months. Remember, stocks which are up strongly early in the trading day, as well as stocks which close strongly, are worth watching. Stocks which do both are especially worth watching.

You may want to consider some of the sector indices very strongly. A sector index, some of which are listed above, will tell you the average value of a group of stocks that are in the same kind of business or related business as the stock you're interested in. Whether it's an oil stock or a computer stock, a biotech stock or a high-tech stock, there's an index for it.

Why look at the sector indices? Because, whether they're doing well or poorly, they'll provide a strong basis of comparison for the stock you're interested in. If the sector is doing well and your stock is not, that tells you something. If the sector is doing well and your stock is doing better, that will tell you something else. Sector analysis tells you both the bullish and bearish outlook for that kind of stock as well as telling you something about how well your stock stacks up against them. It's usually best to buy the strongest stocks in a strong sector and sell the weakest stocks in a weak sector.

Trading Pullbacks

Look for strong stocks whose price is rising and have strong relative strength. Wait for the price to pull back, then dive in and buy. A useful guide to determining if a stock is pulling back is if it doesn't make a new high for three consecutive days. If the sell-off is 5 to 15 percent, that's deep enough so that some stockholders will sell. However, it's not strong enough to panic stockholders into dumping their shares. However, if the stock pulls back 20 percent from its high, watch out. That's a red flag that the price may be headed into a new downtrend.

Don't buy then. Instead, wait for the price to start heading up before placing your order (see Figure 3-21). That way, you'll have made a buy when the stock has some upward momentum, and you'll have refrained from buying if the price keeps falling. Protect yourself with a tight stop order in case you've read the situation incorrectly.

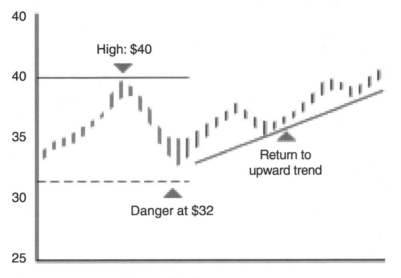

Figure 3-21.   Trading pullback.

Time of Day

The time of day in which you make your trades will have a lot to do to with how successful you are. You've got to take positions which are consistent with each time zone. Just remember that these zones aren't neatly divided, and it takes a lot of practice to see on any particular day when one zone is ending and another is beginning. Each zone has specific qualities. Make sure you exploit them.

9:30 A.M.–9:40 A.M., The Opening.   Thc highest volume and the biggest action is during the first hour, with the final hour a close second. The volume during those two hours combined could reach as high as half of all the volume for the entire day. In fact, highs and lows hit during these two hours often turn out to be the highs or lows for that day. The first hour is basically for the public. However, traders can and do often dive in here. Why? Stocks are at their most volatile then, and the biggest moves happen during the first hour.

The public's enthusiasm, or antagonism, about a particular stock often overwhelms the specialists, who have much greater difficulty keeping an orderly market during the first hour than they do during most of the remainder of the day. That means it's easier to find stocks that are oversold or overbought during the first hour, and a stock may shoot way up or tumble way down to an extent not possible during the rest of the day's trading. There's a good risk-reward ratio here.

However, because the first half hour in particular is so volatile, you should wait until you have about six months' experience before trading during this time. In the meantime, pay close attention during the first half hour of trading to catch its rhythms and its peculiarities. Once you've got enough experience and do start trading then, you'll have a much better idea of what to expect and you'll be able to navigate much better.

During the first hour, you'll see a lot of short-term resistance and support. Testing of trends during the first hour often will set the tone for the rest of the day.

9:40 A.M.–9:45 A.M., The First Pressure Point.   It's at this time that the retail buyers first have access to stock quotes, and their reactions can have a profound effect on a stock's price.

10:00 A.M.–10:35 A.M., The Second Pressure Point.   This time is quite valuable for short-term traders. That's because many traders wait to see how prices came out from the trading between 9:45 and 10:00 A.M. Many day traders wait until this time to determine whether the trend they want to trade will stay intact for the rest of the day.

Trends which survive these two pressure points likely will stay intact for the rest of the day. Many traders rely on the outcome of these two tests more than any other during the day. At this point, volume drops, prices constrict, and range limits are created which are likely to hold up for the rest of the day unless something spectacular happens.

11:00 A.M.–1:00 P.M., Possible Danger Zone.   Traders who buy stocks during these middle hours need to have a clear idea of when they want to get in and when they want to get out. The most important trends to watch here are whether a stock's price veers sharply away from the day's previous close, price range, and total volume. The danger zones here are at 11 A.M. and 1 P.M., the times just before and after lunch. That's when the strongest midday reversals of trends established in the opening hours develop. The 11 A.M. period usually has sharp, short bursts of countertrend activity. At 1 P.M., there may not be much movement. However, if the trend for the day isn't clear, then the people just back from lunch, having taken a break and fueled their energies, may decide to launch a sharp countermove.

On the other hand, if a trend is strongly established, then there's likely to be a sharp move supporting that trend around this time.

The lunch hour itself can be quite tricky. Volume is less, trends are harder to spot, and specialists and market makers play various games to increase volume. Lunchtime is a difficult time to trade, even for veterans. Especially as a beginning trader, you're a lot better off just having lunch. Don't trade during this period. It's too dangerous. Midday traders have to find stocks which have two qualities: They have to have strong trends, and they must have enough volatility to be worth trading. You have to analyze such stocks closely to see if they've broken out of a first-hour range and to figure out what might be good prices to buy the stock. Then you have to decide on your strategy.

At 2:45 P.M., traders closely watch for any sign of a developing trend for any final-hour moves. Then the activity begins.

At 3 P.M., momentum traders are particularly tuned to whether a stock is breaking out of its trading range. There might even be a trend reversal, although that's rare in this time period. You have to know the daily price range and the key resistance and support points to profitably play this hour.

The last 15 minutes can be particularly frenetic, because market movers and many traders close their books based on what they see here. A rush of Market On Close orders can drastically shift spreads and prices. New traders should stay away from trading during this time period. Navigating it is too difficult.

In short, each time of day has its own rhythm, its own opportunities and traps. Short-term traders have to take the market's varying pulse frequently throughout the day, being aware of what it normally would be at that time, and being acutely attuned to any deviations. It's one of the factors that makes short-term trading exciting, dangerous, and, potentially, very profitable.

Technical Analysis
Review Questions
(True/False)

1. As a trader, the high, low, and opening prices have little significance.

2. There are different kinds of gaps.

3. A moving average is a kind of indicator.

4. Comparing how strong or weak a stock is, in relation to a group of stocks or the broader market, is an example of relative strength evaluation.

5. The time of day you trade is of little significance for a day trader.

6. It is a bullish sign for price to increase as volume decreases.

7. In an uptrend, a stock makes higher highs and lower highs.

8. When a support level is broken, that level now becomes the new resistance level.

Technical Analysis Review Answers

1. False
2. True
3. True
4. True
5. False
6. False
7. False
8. True

FUNDAMENTAL ANALYSIS

What Is Fundamental Analysis?

THE OTHER HALF OF THE ANALYSIS EQUATION is *fundamental analysis.* What's the difference between technical and fundamental analysis? Fundamental analysts focus on the company, its own economic circumstances, and the economic circumstances in which the company operates. It does not peer into the gyrations of the stock. Instead, it focuses on the nuts and bolts of the company and the economy to establish the value of a company and to predict what a company's stock should sell for.

Even though fundamental analysis generally is used by people with a longer-term trading horizon, traders such as yourself need it, too. The more information you have about a stock and the company it represents, the better. It can only help you, even if you are a day trader. The longer your time frame—and that means even if you're a swing trader on a 2- to 5-day cycle—the more important it is to use fundamental analysis. The longer your time frame, the more likely it is that the trend you spotted will materialize.

Although technical analysis usually leads fundamental, it is best to also find fundamental support for your trading ideas. Traders should use both technical *and* fundamental analysis, because together they will give you the best information available and will stack the odds in your favor.

Having the most complete information rounds out your picture of what influences are playing on a stock that you hold or that you might hold.

Fundamental analysts care about the nature of the economy and the nature of the company. They examine reports about the part of the economy in which the company operates and the economy in general. Fundamental analysts also want to know the details of a specific company's financial position and its management, as well as how economic indicators are likely to affect the circumstances under which the company operates. Remember, though, that when you're trading, when you get in and when you get out matter a lot. Fundamental analysis often is broad in its scope, and it does not tell you when to buy and when to sell. Technical analysis helps us time a trade.

However, fundamental analysis will tell you what the broad economic forces playing upon your individual stocks and the entire market might be. Whether the forces are in a positive or negative direction, your style of trading should match the trend, whether it's bullish or bearish.

Here's what fundamental analysis tries to do: it tries to predict the future direction of the market as a whole, and it tries to predict the direction of stocks you own now and may own in the future. Fundamental analysis has a large number of methods to check on the economy or stocks. In this chapter, you'll be introduced to a few of those techniques.

The Economy

Let's break down these various categories into specifics. First, let's look at how fundamentalists examine the bigger picture, the economic environment in which a company operates. There are several indicators fundamentalists regularly look at:

- **The Dollar.** If the dollar is strong, that means imports into this country will be cheap because the dollar is worth so much more. That fact squeezes inflation down, but American industries which rely on exporting get hurt because exports will be more expensive. A weaker dollar means American manufacturers will be helped, because their goods will be cheaper overseas, but it also may boost inflation.

- **Interest Rates.** This is the price institutions pay to borrow money. These rates are governed by the Federal Reserve, or Fed, as it is known, because only that governing board can set interest rates between institutions. When short-term rates are lower than long-term, the Fed is trying to give the economy a boost. When short-term rates are higher than long-term, the Fed is trying to make more expensive the acquisition of money to expand or improve businesses, so the economy will slow down. Note: Rising interest rates are considered to be bearish. When interest rates rise, the stocks hardest hit initially will be high price to earnings (P-E) stocks (because the value of their future earnings decreases), high-flying technology stocks, Internet stocks, banks, and carmakers.

- **Inventory.** This number includes how much a company's raw materials, work in progress, supplies, and finished goods on hand are worth. If a company isn't selling its goods, then it has more inventory than it should. The price of that inventory has to be reduced to clear it out, and that means less money coming in for the company to buy new products and hire consultants, for instance. Fundamentalists are interested in the U.S. Commerce Department's mid-month number comparing the amount of sales nationally to business inventory.

- **Labor Costs.** Basically, this is the cost of having employees. The Bureau of Labor Statistics figures a quarterly employment cost index, which the *Wall Street Journal* faithfully reports.

- **Leading Indicators.** A monthly merging of 12 indicators compiled by the Commerce Department's Bureau of Economic Analysis. Many fundamentalists think this statistic shows where the economy will be in several months.

- **Productivity.** This number shows how much the average worker produces. It's easiest to measure in the manufacturing arena, because the basic measure there is the number of units per worker. When productivity is on the way up, companies can pay workers more money and still not have to raise prices.

- **Real Gross Domestic Product (GDP).** This number shows the value of goods and services produced by property and people in the United States. The Commerce Department releases these figures quarterly.

- **Unemployment Rate.** This number is the percentage of the civilian work force which doesn't have a job and is actively trying to find one.

- **Consumer Confidence.** A monthly statistic issued by the Conference Board. If the number is up, the economy probably is headed that way. If it's down, then the economy could be in trouble.

- **Personal Income.** If people are making more money, they'll spend more money. If they're making less money, they'll spend less. This statistic comes from the Commerce Department

- **Consumer Price Index (CPI).** This indicator measures the rate at which consumer prices go up or down for food, housing, transportation, medical care, clothing electricity, services, and entertainment.

Fundamentalists believe that each of these indicators could be a cause which should have a specific result when it rises or falls, though there may be an exception. For example:

1. If interest rates increase, then economic growth should slow down because the cost of doing business has gone up, so projects which wouldn't make a lot of money will be cancelled. However, the increases may not be enough to put the brakes on growth.

2. If the dollar decreases, or weakens, then the economy should pick up because the price of goods is cheaper overseas, resulting in increased exports because consumers will be drawn to the lowered prices. However, all may not be well. The trade barriers put up by other countries may make exporting to those countries difficult, or consumers in other countries may think that, regardless of price, American goods are second-rate.

3. If unemployment rises, then fewer people have money to spend and the economy doesn't grow as quickly. To stimulate the economy, the Fed may ease credit, allowing companies to get money cheaper so they can start more projects or build up staff. That would reduce unemployment.

4. If the *Gross Domestic Product* (GDP) rises, that means the economy is picking up steam and the Fed may tighten the money supply by raising interest rates if it thinks the economy is growing too rapidly.

5. If inventories increase, the economy is slowing because people, organizations, and companies aren't buying things as quickly as they're being produced.

Just remember, these illustrations are only a few of the many scenarios which could play out. And you must keep firmly in mind that these scenarios are guidelines, and guidelines only. They are not magic formulas or rigorous science which will let you predict with absolute certainty what will happen. They work sometimes, and that's why they're worth knowing about. They don't work all the time, and you shouldn't expect them to.

The Business Cycle

Fundamentalists use the preceding indicators and others to assess what phase the economy is in as part of what's called the business cycle or the liquidity cycle. It has to do with the economy expanding and contracting. Each cycle generally runs from three to four years and has four distinct phases. See Figure 4-1.

The business cycle is shown below.

1. *Trough.* This is when the economy is at its worst. It's when business activity hits rock-bottom. Almost every economic measure is down: gross domestic product, industrial production, and productivity. It's a very bad time.

2. *Recovery.* Business activity increases. The Dow Jones Industrial Average, consumer confidence, and sales of all kinds of things are all starting to move up. People and business have more money to spend than when the economy is in a trough.

The Business Cycle

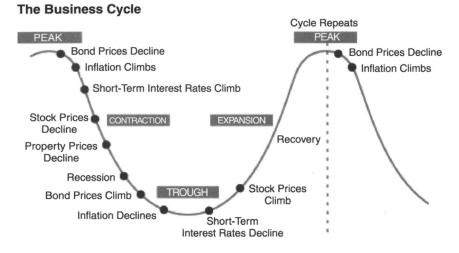

Figure 4-1. The business cycle, also known as the liquidity cycle.

3. *Peak.* Here is the economy at its most vibrant. Economists also call this stage prosperity. Gross domestic product, productivity, consumer confidence, personal income, and almost every other measure is at its top.

4. *Contraction.* Now starts the slide downhill. Business activity begins to decline. The consumer price index is up, but personal income, consumer confidence, and sales of all types are sliding downward. Contractions come in two strengths: mild and strong. Recessions are mild contractions lasting two to six consecutive quarters; depressions are when business activity declines last longer than six quarters.

Some of the most popular signs of a rising economy are rising stock markets, increased consumer demand, and an increased GDP. A slowing economy is reflected by falling stock markets, decreasing GDP, and decreased consumer demand.

Remember, this cycle is not a natural phenomenon subject solely to the whims of the marketplace. The Federal Reserve Board has a truly fundamental impact on how these phases play out. The Fed's function, as described by its current chairman, Alan Greenspan, is to take away the punch bowl just when the party is getting started.

But the Fed also hauls out the punch bowl and tries to throw a party when the economy starts getting glum.

How? The Fed raises interest rates if it thinks the economy is getting too strong (this is the part about taking away the punch bowl), and that means money is less available for business because money costs more. If the Fed thinks the economy needs prodding, then it cuts back interest rates. That means borrowing money is cheaper, and more businesses will be started or expanded as a result.

Of course, the Fed doesn't have a magic wand, and the effects of its moves sometimes are delayed or simply don't work. However, what the Fed does is one of the most important aspects of any analysis of the overall economy.

The Fed isn't the only governmental influence here. Government —state, local, and federal—can raise or lower taxes, and that move alone could have a big impact on the economy. Usually, it's the federal government's moves in this area which have the most impact, the same with budget surpluses and deficits. Governmental deficits mean, among other things, that interest has to be paid which could be put to other uses.

Surpluses mean that politicians will put the money to work for projects, give the money back to taxpayers, pay off debt, start new programs, or use the money to shore up financially ailing programs. All of these moves have effects on the economy.

Deflation, Inflation, and Stagflation

There are three different price situations to which you should pay very close attention; the Fed certainly does. They are deflation, inflation, and stagflation. None of them are pleasant.

Deflation, the opposite of inflation, is when prices go down and keep going down. That doesn't mean people will go on a buying spree. Quite the opposite, in fact. Production of goods and services usually outstrips demand, probably because unemployment also goes up. During inflation, prices generally go up and keep going up. Usually this happens when the economy is expanding and employment is high. When stagflation hits, the economy has the worst of both worlds. It offers a sour soup of high unemployment (stagflation) and high rising prices (inflation).

Defensive, Cyclical, and Growth Industries

Some kinds of industries are more sensitive to the business cycle than others. You should be aware of the nature of the industry the company is part of. There are three different kinds: defensive, cyclical, and growth.

Defensive industries are the goods and services that people consider to be necessities in good times and bad. That means when the business cycle turns down, they don't get hit as hard and their stocks are less risky. Such stocks would include health care, food, drug, and energy. Cyclical companies go up and down with the business cycle, and when times are bad their business suffers. These stocks include any businesses in construction and related industries, such as heavy equipment, and raw materials, such as cement, steel, and paper. Growth companies are any stocks which are growing faster than the economy. Don't expect a lot of dividends from these companies, because they're putting all their earnings into expansion.

One important piece of information about growth companies is how long the company has been in business. Growth industries fall into several categories, often depending on how long they and the industry have been around. If they're solid companies in an industry which has existed for a long time, then they're a pretty safe bet, but don't expect a lot of earnings growth. These companies use their cash to pay dividends or for diversification, which may or may not succeed. If they're new companies in an industry which has been around a long time, that's getting riskier. They had better offer something very different from their competitors, and that something special should be highly prized by prospective customers. And if it's a new company in a new industry, watch out. That's as risky as it gets, and the company's technology had better be tops.

Beta

It's not just the economy and the kind of company involved that fundamentalists want to know about. They also want to know how well a company's stock does in comparison to the rest of the market. That measure is called *beta*. A stock which has a beta of 1 goes up and down precisely the way the overall market is doing. A stock with a beta of 2 is twice as sensitive to market ups and downs as the market itself. Stocks with a beta of higher than 1 are called *aggressive* stocks, and are the ones most favored by traders. Stocks which have a beta of less than 1 don't move up and down as much as the market itself, and stocks which move independently of the market have in theory a beta of 0. Such stocks are called *defensive,* because they dampen the market's gyrations.

The Company's Financial Position

Fundamental analysts want to make sure the company they're considering has two important qualities: growth and stability. The kind of information about the company these analysts scrutinize includes:

- **The balance sheet.** This information shows the company's assets and liabilities. Make sure the total assets equal the total liabilities.
- **The profit and loss statement.** This information shows the income, costs, and expenses of a company over a given period of time. You're looking for the net profit, after all the liabilities have been accounted for.

The most important piece of financial information about the company a fundamental analyst is looking for is earnings—specifically what their future direction might be. Here are the issues:

1. Earnings
    a. Are they going up or down each year, adjusted for inflation?
    b. Have they been good in the past long enough to feel confident they're likely to be good in the future?
    c. How big is the return on the stock compared to how much you invest?
    d. Do the earnings compare well to the whole economy?
    e. Do the earnings compare well to other companies in the same sector?
2. How much is the company worth?
3. What kind of accounting has the company used to calculate its earnings?

Crash Course

Here's a crash course in the various ways of figuring earnings that you'll need to know. You will see here a few calculations which you've done before. You'll be seeing them again because it's important for you to know how earnings work in fundamental analysis, because earnings are essential to understanding fundamental analysis.

To show how these calculations work, let's take an example: a company has issued 20 million shares, has earnings of $40 million this year and the directors have decided to pay out a $10 million dividend. Right now, the company is trading at $48 a share.

1. Earnings per share (EPS) = Earnings/Shares issued = 40,000,000/20,000,000 = $2/share.

   EPS helps you compare an individual stock in two ways: to others in its same industry or sector and also to the stock's price, to see if the stock is a good buy. Incidentally, you've got to adjust this figure if the number of shares outstanding changes during the year. Then you have to use a weighted average, which takes the change in the number of shares into account.

   Suppose a company had 50,000 shares outstanding at the beginning of the fiscal year, then, six months into the fiscal year, had a rights issue of 5000 shares. That's when a company offers existing stockholders the right to buy more stock. The stockholders can take up the offer or sell their rights in the marketplace. In addition, let's suppose the company had $100,000 in earnings.

   To get the weighted average for this company, you take into account how long each share was available:

   Weighted average = [(50,000 × 12 months) + (5000 × 6 months)]/12 = (600,000 + 30,000)/12 = 630,000/12 = 52,500 shares.

   So, earnings per share would be $100,000/52,500 = $1.90 per share.

2. Price-earnings ratio (P-E) = Price/EPS = $48/2 = 24 = 24 to 1.

   The P-E ratio is another method of comparison. It's a barometer many traders use to compare one stock against another and to compare how well a stock is doing against both the overall market and its own industry group. By the way, a high P-E ratio is not necessarily a good sign. In fact, it's often an indication that the stock's price is not a bargain anymore and may even be over-priced. A stock with a very low P-E often is considered by the market to have a future in which earnings will slump from their current levels.

Here's an example: If Motorola were trading at 140 and had a P-E ratio of 36, while the S&P 500 had a market P-E ratio of 31, then Motorola would be considered a little more expensive than the market average. Remember, though, that growth stocks have high P-Es compared to their growth rate.

Please note: The picture has become more complicated. The pro-longed bull market has produced much higher-priced stocks, and the Internet stocks are carrying very high prices even though they have no earnings. These developments mean that you have to be a little more cautious when using P-E as part of your trading strategy.

3. Earnings yield (EY) = EPS/Price × 100 = 2/48 × 100 = 4.16 %. This figure will let you compare what the price offers you com-pared to current bank CD rates. Remember, this comparison is only a rule of thumb. You can't compare them directly because the earnings yield is a measure of what's happened in the recent past but is no guarantee of the future. Bank CD rates are a promise to pay a certain rate for a specified time during the future.

Earnings Momentum

Earnings are essential for fundamental analysis, because what you're looking for is earnings momentum, where a company's earn-ings consistently increase from one quarter to another, one year to another. A company with earnings up 18 percent in one year and 27 percent the next year has earnings momentum. Many professionals in the stock market look for stocks which have earnings increases of at least 20 percent during each of three quarters.

If a company's earnings record is spotty—up 20 percent one year, down 12 percent the next year, up 30 percent the next year, and up 5 percent the year after, for example—that's a negative. Earnings surprises can be positive or negative.

If the company's earnings reports beat the estimates analysts projected, that's a good sign for the stock. If the company's actual earnings fall below expectations, then the stock's price will fall. Incidentally, take note of a company's debt. If it's at a very high level, then even a small earnings downturn could cause the stock price to tumble.

Also, take note of how well a company historically meets or beats the stock analysts' estimates of earnings. Two sources of these estimates are First Call and Zack's. If the analysts following that stock have to revise their estimates downward, then the stock may do poorly for that quarter. Of course, if analysts keep having to revise their earnings estimates upward, then the stock may be expected to announce good numbers.

By the way, take note of the *whisper number*. That's the earnings estimate the stock analyst community is actually using for a stock, but won't say so publicly. Analysts publish official estimates, and the aggregate of all the analysts' official speculations is called the consensus number. But then analysts hint, through the whisper number, at what they think the real story will be.

Why do analysts have a whisper number? Because companies play games, offering earnings forecasts which are often low, making it easy for the real earnings to beat the forecasts. In fact, most companies do better than the official analyst forecasts. For example, in a recent quarter, almost two-thirds of American companies beat what the analysts predicted, while just 12 percent fell short.

Because they know that companies are low-balling estimates, analysts speculate on what they think the genuine earnings story is, resulting in the whisper numbers. You can find whisper numbers on Internet sites such as thewhispernumber.com, whispernumber.com, and jagnotes.com. Because most companies do beat the consensus number, if a stock can't even beat what everybody in the business knows is an artificially low number, then, the theory goes, watch out! The company must have some serious problems.

The whisper numbers recently gained credibility when two Midwestern university professors found that whisper numbers are more accurate than consensus numbers in predicting earnings.

When you throw in the whisper number, you have three numbers to deal with: the official estimate, the whisper number, and the actual published earnings. If a company beats the whisper number, that's a plus. Not too surprisingly, a company which doesn't meet or beat the whisper number, even if it beats the consensus number, may watch its stock price fall.

However, even if a company does beat both numbers, that's not the end of the story. If the company at the same time warns that its growth might slow down or that its revenues will fall short of projections, that's a danger sign, too. The Street generally will react to the negative news, rather than the positive, and the stock price will suffer.

Know when a company will report its earnings through Zack's, First Call, and other sources. Then watch for any unusual trading during the weeks before the report comes out. This period, which happens during the four times each year that companies report their earnings, is cause for great worry among analysts, traders, investors, fund managers, and others. They are concerned about whether a company will meet or exceed its earnings projections, and they will put money into that stock or pull money out, depending on their reading of the situation.

That unusual trading might be an indication of whether to expect an earnings surprise, in which the company's earnings either fall short of, or are better than, what analysts had predicted.

Remember, as companies begin to report earnings, companies which are related to each other will show stock price increases or decreases, depending on the earnings reports of the first few companies related to them. If Wal-Mart and Kmart both have bad earnings reports, stocks in the discount retail sector could be in for a tough ride.

In addition, when larger companies report their earnings, the stock price of related companies will often go up or down along with the earnings reports of those companies. If IBM reports bad earnings, then the price of Compaq might go down, too.

Here's a basic tip: avoid stocks whose earnings patterns are too wild or don't have any pattern you can see. You can't predict where those stocks will go. If you buy these stocks, you're doing nothing more than gambling.

Market Capitalization

You need to know how much a company is worth so you know which companies are about the same size for purposes of comparison. To find out how big the company is, which is another way of saying how much it's worth, you'll want to use the market capitalization calculation.

Here's how it works: number of shares outstanding × price = 20,000,000 × 45 = $900,000,000. That's how much the market thinks this company is worth at this time.

Risk

There are many kinds of risk, and you need to factor all of them into your fundamental analysis of a stock and the economy.

Probably the biggest risk is losing all your money (capital risk). That could happen because you simply lose all your invested capital, or the company goes bankrupt and your stock loses most or all of its value (credit risk). Then there are risks that are simply part of being in the market: you might not be able to buy or sell the amount of stock you want (liquidity risk), you might buy or sell at the wrong time (timing risk), or the market might go down, taking the value of your stocks with it (market risk).

Accounting

Even when you're comparing the earnings of companies with similar P-Es, the companies may not be as identical as you think. Why? The companies may have used different accounting methods. The Securities and Exchange Commission requires that companies disclose certain matters about how well the business has done during and at the end of its financial year. But there are lots of areas which are not clear. They fall into a category called *Generally Accepted Accounting Principles* (GAAP).

One of these principles is that companies have to be conservative in how they value assets and liabilities. If the company can't pin down precisely the value of an asset or the amount of money coming in, the company should understate that asset or income, not overstate it. On the other hand, if the company has a liability or an expense which can't be figured out precisely, the company is supposed to overstate the value. The problem is, those accounting principles don't spell out exactly how much a company is supposed to understate or overstate, so there's leeway, and some companies take advantage of that fact more than others. The result: companies can vary considerably in how they make these calculations.

When you look at a company's figures, try to figure out how conservative they are. For example, a highly conservative company might understate its earnings; if you didn't know that fact, your earnings comparisons with other companies that take a more liberal approach might be misleading. However, the more conservative the accounting practices, the more you can rely on the earnings that company reports.

Management

This area is quite tricky, but it's essential to fundamental analysis. Why? Because it's that management team which is making the key decisions about what to do with the company's resources and its cash.

Figuring out the quality of management is difficult when you rely on other people, because you must be sure those people know what they're talking about. Your best bet is to do some of the work on your own, using an organization chart. Pay particular attention to the people at the very top, such as the chief executive officer and the board of directors. Find and clip articles written about them. Financial magazines often do profiles on such people.

If the company has some kind of operation near you, go see it. See how well you think it's being managed. Many companies will happily show you the facilities and answer your questions. If you can get time alone with some employees, ask them individually how they feel about some of the important managers. You might be surprised at the answers.

Comb through the company's annual reports. Board chairmen and directors often spell out how well they think the company will do financially during the next year. Look over past annual reports and see how well their previous predictions have held up. Incidentally, the best source for fundamental analysis of company reports is Edgar-Online.

News

As a trader who uses fundamental analysis, you need new trading ideas. That means you need to know what's happening to the stocks you're considering, as well as the stocks you're already holding and the economy as a whole. You need to stay fastened to the news. In fact, before the market opens you should be going through a routine which will keep you current on the news. Staying current makes you more profitable, or at least prevents you from losing a lot of money because there was news you didn't know: a new top manager may be in or out, a company is bringing out a new product or dropping an old one, a division is being opened or closed.

The news possibilities are endless, and most of them will help or hurt your stocks. Just remember this: the announcements of changes in policy or personnel, and the expectations of those changes, matter a lot to your trading. Remember the saying, "Buy on rumor, sell on news." You need to be up-to-the-minute on both rumors and news.

Generally, if there's good news, such as a company being a takeover candidate, a stock's price will go up on the rumor. Then, if and when the rumor becomes fact, generally the stock will start to sell off on that good news. That rule of thumb doesn't happen 100 percent of the time, of course.

Know, however, that there are different kinds of news sources. Take your stock news from mainstream sources, not from Internet chat rooms. Here is a list of sources and publications which are worth your time.

Print publications include: *Barron's, Fortune, Individual Investor, Investor's Business Daily, Moody's, New York Times, Smart Money, Standard & Poor's* stock reports, and the *Wall Street Journal.* Don't forget books and professional newsletters and publications, too. Broadcast sources include Bloomberg, Nightly Business Report (PBS), CNBC, CNN, as well as Lew Rukeyser's Wall Street Week.

You have to be especially careful on the Internet, because many sources are not reliable. However, there are several which can be helpful, including America Online, Briefing.com, CBS/Marketwatch, Motley Fool, and theStreet.com.

Remember, information is essential to your strategy. You must know what is going on in the market, in the economy, in the world, in order to make the best possible judgments as to what are the best stocks to buy and sell. Without news, your strategy has no eyes, no ears, no sense. For the sake of fattening your profits, feed yourself a daily diet of news.

Several kinds of news could affect a stock's price immediately. Earnings are very important, whether it's a surprise or a report. A new invention, product, or service usually is good news, and you should particularly watch approval or rejection from the Food and Drug Administration in the biotech field. FDA announcements are very important. So is an arrangement with another well-known company, whether it's some kind of deal, a merger, or an acquisition. If the market thinks the new arrangement will work, then the stocks of both companies will go up. If the market doesn't like the new combination, both stocks could take a hit. For example, when America Online announced it was buying Time-Warner, the market hated the idea and AOL's stock lost 20 percent in just a few days.

There's one final piece of news which, while it doesn't move stocks as dramatically as the previously mentioned catalysts, certainly is a fundamental factor you need to be aware of and one which does move a stock price. It's analysts' revisions. The revision can be a stock upgrade or downgrade, earnings revisions upward or downward, and stock price revisions upward or downward.

You should know, however, that you need to treat the enthusiasm of analysts with your own skepticism. Analysts generally work for companies which do underwriting for stock offerings. That fact means that often the analysts are under pressure from their employers not to be as skeptical as they should about the stocks they cover, especially if the employer has underwritten a stock offering for that stock. Test out this information for yourself: most analysts use either categories or numbers to describe their enthusiasm or lack of it. The categories go something like this: strong buy, buy, accumulate, hold, sell. If it's a number system, 1 = strong buy, 2 = buy, 3 = accumulate, 4 = hold, 5 = sell. The first three are considered bullish, while the last two are bearish.

The next time you check on stocks, see how many analysts actually recommend holding or selling one. You'll find that, at most, 10 percent of analysts' recommendations are bearish. For that reason, an analyst's issuing an outright sell recommendation is quite significant, and you should give it an extra measure of weight.

The rating by an analyst at a big brokerage such as Goldman Sachs is more important than what an analyst from a small brokerage might say. In addition, if any analyst upgrades or downgrades a stock more than one category, for example, going from a 3 rating to a 1 rating, that's a significant sign.

Furthermore, if any analyst had an upgrade or a downgrade of the stock accompanied by an earnings revision, up or down, or a change in the price targets, up or down, those are significant signs.

And finally, be aware of and avoid the often insignificant reiterated buy rating.

Fundamental Analysis Review Questions

Choose the corresponding letter for each stock type. A letter can be used more than once.

1. Paper stocks
2. Technology stocks
3. Energy stocks
4. Steel stocks
5. Food stocks
6. Drug stocks

A. Cyclical stock
B. Defensive stock
C. Growth stock

7. When interest rates rise, stock prices are likely to
   a. rise
   b. fall
   c. hold steady
   d. rise, then fall

8. Deflation is when
   a. prices go up and keep going up
   b. prices go down and keep going down
   c. prices hold steady
   d. prices go down and then go up

9. Inflation usually occurs when
   a. the economy is expanding, employment is high, and prices are going down
   b. the economy is expanding, employment is high, and prices are going up

   c. the economy is expanding, employment is low, and prices are going up

   d. the economy is contracting, employment is low, and prices are going up

10. Stagflation is when there is
   a. low unemployment and low falling prices
   b. low unemployment and high rising prices
   c. high unemployment and low rising prices
   d. high unemployment and high rising prices

11. A stock with a beta of 2 would indicate that
   a. the stock's volatility is in concert with the overall market
   b. the stock's volatility is greater than the overall market
   c. the stock's volatility is less than the overall market
   d. the stock's volatility is two times less than the overall market

Part I General Review Questions

1. An investor would short a stock when he or she thinks
   a. interest rates will decrease
   b. a price will increase
   c. a price will decrease
   d. a price will double

2. When would you use a sell limit order?
   a. to sell a long stock position if the market rises
   b. to sell a short stock position if the market rises
   c. to sell a long stock position if the market falls
   d. to sell a short stock position if the market falls

3. When would you use a sell stop order?
   a. to limit a loss on a long stock position
   b. to limit a loss on a short stock position
   c. to limit a loss on either a long or short stock position
   d. to cancel a sell order

4. A market maker
   a. functions as an agent
   b. must sell when there are no other sellers
   c. functions as a principal
   d. must own a seat on the NYSE

5. An order to buy stock at a specific price is a
   a. market order
   b. limit order
   c. stop limit order
   d. stop order

6. The broadest market index is
   a. The Dow Jones Industrial Average
   b. Standard & Poor's 500
   c. The Value Line Index
   d. The Wilshire Index

7. Beta measures
   a. stock volatility based on specific characteristics of a company
   b. capital risk
   c. timing risk
   d. stock volatility based on general market movements

8. Can a trader buy short?
   a. yes
   b. no

9. Outstanding stock is
   a. stock that is repurchased shares
   b. stock that has a fixed number of shares issued
   c. stock that is in the public's hands
   d. stock that is considered a blue-chip security

10. What does it mean to sell short?
    a. sell securities that you own
    b. sell borrowed securities
    c. sell securities short of your limit price
    d. sell securities short of your stop order

11. A dealer cannot
    a. act as a principal on one side of a transaction
    b. make a market
    c. provide a firm offer to sell a stock
    d. back away from a quote

Fundamental Analysis Review Answers

1. A
2. C
3. B
4. A
5. B
6. B
7. B
8. B
9. B
10. D
11. B

Part I General Review Answers

1. C
2. A
3. A
4. C
5. B
6. D
7. D
8. B
9. C
10. B
11. D

THE STRATEGIES
OF TRADING

THE NEXT THREE CHAPTERS TELL YOU how to put into motion all the theory that you've been learning. No doubt some of you skipped all of that information and headed straight for these chapters first. If that's what you did, it was a mistake.

Please understand that trading strategies will do you no good all by themselves. You must grasp all the material that has come before it so you can fashion your personal strategy in a way that will make you the most money. The next three chapters are meant to give you a number of different ways to use that strategy.

You will learn several methods to analyze the market and execute trades. You should not use these strategies in isolation from each other. The most successful short-term traders are those who combine several strategies. When you merge more than one strategy, and add technical and fundamental analysis, you stack the odds more heavily in your favor. For example, if you combine chart patterns with news about an individual stock, your strategy will be better-informed and more sound than if you used just chart patterns or news.

Remember, there is no magic bullet, no specific formula, which will make you a successful short-term trader. It takes a great deal of work and research. There's no way around it. In addition, you have to develop your own approach, using at the very least the information you find here, along with money management and discipline. The real test will be when you start diving into the market using your own money. When you do, you will start to refine and hone your personal strategy. Your strategy may be quite sound at the beginning, but no matter how good it is, it will need tweaking. Tweaking takes time, and time often means losing money.

When you're a swing trader, if something goes significantly against you, then it's best to sell it or, if you're short, buy it back the next morning after the first hour of trading. Most beginning traders will hold onto their losers hoping they will bounce back, while selling their winners when just a glimmer of a profit emerges. Better to sell your losers and buy them back at a lower price and hold your winners. You must dump your losers if they're down significantly, because if you don't, your losses will probably only get worse.

Losing money, especially at the beginning, is not a badge of shame. It is part of the tuition you're paying to get your education in the market. Even the best traders have slumps, and you will, too. Remember, if you use strong discipline and sound money-management principles, you will be able to ride through those rough patches, which are inevitable in trading, just as they are in any kind of business.

When you look over these strategies, you will see that some of them are similar. That's alright. The idea is to make your personal strategy as subtle or as rich as you want. A shade of difference in that strategy may suit your personal approach, which won't be the way someone else wants to run their account, even though both of you may decide that the broad principle involved is important to include in how you deploy your money.

Before we move on to the specifics of each strategy, here's an overall money management tip: you're better off buying stocks when they pull back. Even the hottest stocks do inevitably pull back, at least for a little while, and buying stocks on the downswing is a lot cheaper than catching a rocket's tail while it's headed straight up. So, buy strong stocks sitting still or on dips, and short weak stocks on bounces or sitting still. Do not buy stocks after they have spiked up, nor short stocks after they have broken down.

When you read about these strategies, don't just analyze them for how well they might fit into the way you want to trade in the market. Do a gut check—repeatedly. If you're comfortable with an approach, then it deserves further consideration. If you're uncomfortable with it, no matter how slightly, then drop it from your arsenal. A strategy has to be both intellectually and emotionally attractive. You will spend many hours a day, for months, even years on end, executing and refining your trading strategy. That's too much and too long a time to spend with a method you don't really like, for whatever reason. If your gut says no, then drop it.

Here is another tip right at the beginning: trade the NYSE and Nasdaq differently. You're basically going against the trend as a NYSE trader. There, you should buy on weakness and sell on strength. For Nasdaq, buy on strength and sell on weakness; you're always using momentum. If a stock is down 12 points for the day, you can feel much better about buying it at that point if it's a listed stock.

For the NYSE stocks, you're trying to figure out when selling or buying has reached its conclusion. When the stock has reached a point where either selling or buying is pretty much exhausted, you can expect a short-term bounce in the other direction. That's what short-term trading of listed stocks is about. You have to figure out when the selling is over and the short-term bounce back has begun.

As you know, the NYSE has specialists whose job it is to keep the markets orderly. They are the people who apply brakes to the system. For that reason, it's very unusual for a stock to go straight up. If a stock does, for example, rise eight points in a day or two, the odds are high that it will fall. Instead of waiting for a pullback, look for reasons to sell that stock short.

Nasdaq can be harder to read because there are many games being played by market makers. Information from the Nasdaq market just isn't as reliable as information from the Big Board. You might not hit as many homeruns on the NYSE as the Nasdaq, but there is a good chance you'll do better overall because the volatility is less, and your losses and risk will be smaller. If you're wrong, you can control the loss because the range may only be several points and there aren't huge run-ups. On Nasdaq, if you lose, you could lose very, very big.

We can also trade the NYSE in a defensive manner. We know our risk, how much we can lose, before we enter a trade because we can employ stops. This also fits in with our philosophy: first, learn not to lose money, so that eventually you can make money.

For Nasdaq, your short-term trading strategy should be to ride the elevator when a stock is heading upward. That's called buying strength. As the Nasdaq stock price rises, hold off your buy until the price temporarily drops. That's called waiting for a pullback. It takes great discipline to hold off buying when the stock seems to be zooming straight up, and sometimes you will miss what turns out to be a good opportunity. Even so, most often, even the sharpest rises have pullbacks, and that's when you should buy.

Overall, trading is becoming more difficult. In addition to increasing competition, there is more and louder market news, and the market's own reaction to it makes for increased volatility within sessions. Also, in the past there was no overnight domestic stock market. Now there is. There will be other changes in the future, some of them almost unimaginable now. In short, the old fixed rules apply only for the time they exist, and you can't expect them to last forever. You have to be prepared to adjust your strategy when the rules change, and you have to be ready to use every method at your disposal to alter your own approach. You have to have the versatility of a craftsman. Just as they have to pick the appropriate tool for the job, so do you.

We must treat each day differently. Just as a quarterback might adjust his play-calling based on the defense the other team is using on that particular play, we must read and recognize the ever-changing market and adjust our strategies accordingly. We must learn to balance and combine strategies. By learning to use technical and fundamental analysis, different trading strategies, and risk management, we should be able to develop the necessary flexibility and strategies to compete in the market.

C H A P T E R

STRATEGIES: THE OVERNIGHT TRADING SYSTEM[1]

T he *Overnight Trading System* (OTS) is a unique core trading strategy outlined in *The On-Site Trading, Inc. Training Manual*. It can be used as a foundation for developing additional trading techniques. It is a trend-following system that takes advantage of the momentum from close to open. It is a system designed to capture momentum on both the upside and the downside on stocks held overnight. Volume, price change, daily range, and recent trends are the best short-term indicators.

[1] Source: Based on the system as outlined in *The On-Site Trading, Inc. Training Manual*.

This system is based on four fundamental principles of trading:

1. Cut losses and let winners run.
2. Momentum is a good predictor of future stock movement.
3. Always trade with the trend.
4. Money management is essential.

It is up to you to follow the rules. Most traders do not last because of a lack of discipline. There may be periods of time when the system might not work well. As with any system, you must know when to be aggressive and when to be conservative to effectively maximize profits and minimize losses.

The System

Traders must:

1. Trade a minimum of six to eight positions daily. Ideally, eight to 12 positions or more are optimal.
2. Diversify over a large sampling of trades across and within market sectors. This technique is most successful in trending markets. It is more effective to spread your risk by taking more positions.
3. Always hedge your exposure to large unexpected market moves.

General Guidelines

Here are the general guidelines for stock selection.

1. Query for overnight long and short positions every hour beginning at 2:00 P.M. The criterion for this list includes stocks up or down at least three-quarters of a point from their close and within a quarter of a point of their daily high or low with percentage average daily volume above average. Volume for potential short positions is not as important as volume for potential long positions.
2. Look to see which stocks have earnings due within the next three days, then eliminate those stocks. Filter out stocks whose move was based on a news-related event specific to the stock or whose

range is less than one-half point for the day. Also, filter out stocks that look over- or underextended. If news occurred late in the trading session and that stock continues its trend into the close, then this may be a very strong overnight candidate. If the news occurred earlier and the trend continues, it may still be a strong overnight position.

3. Look for strong stocks in strong industry groups or weak stocks in weak industry groups. Eliminate weak stocks in strong industry groups or strong stocks in weak industry groups. If a few stocks in one industry group are potential overnight candidates, then look at the rest of the group to see what else is strong or weak. The later the move occurs, the better the trade.

4. Narrow the list down to stocks which qualify based on the aforementioned criteria.

5. Keep checking each hour after 2:00 P.M. to find any new stock candidates. Also, make sure that the stocks that you have already qualified are still viable.

6. Between 2:50 and 4:00 P.M., begin to trade the list of stocks selectively. It is very important to look at market conditions to see which direction the market will close. For example, put on long positions if the market looks strong. Gauge the momentum of the market and the futures toward the close. Enter short positions into a short covering retracement closer to 4:00 P.M. Weigh long versus short by market condition and how you might expect the market to open the following day. Watch new highs or lows that also meet the overnight criteria.

Entry Rules for Overnight Positions

Below are some guidelines for initiating a stock purchase or short sale that are candidates to hold overnight.

	Stocks <$25	Stocks $25–60	Stocks >$60
Entry time	2:50–4:00 P.M.	3:00–4:00 P.M.	3:30–4:00 P.M.
Suggested size	2 lots	1 lot	1 lot
	(½ 2:50–3:15 P.M.)		

continues

	Stocks <$25 (½ if moving your way)	Stocks $25–60	Stocks >$60
Entry rule long	Up >⅝	Up >¾	Up >⅞
	¼ off high	¼ off high	⅜ off high
	Upper ⅓ range →		
Entry rule short	Down >⅝	Down >¾	Down >⅞
	Bottom ⅓ range →		
Volume long	>1 × 5-day moving average →		
Volume short	>.5 × 5-day moving average →		

Exit Rules for Overnight Positions

Below are some guidelines for closing out a stock purchase or short sale held from the previous trading day.

	Stocks <$25	Stocks $25–60	Stocks >$60
Exit rule long	½ off high	⅝ off high	¾ off high
Exit rule short	½ off low	⅝ off low	¾ off low

The key to OTS is allowing time for the stock to continue its momentum into the following day. Before closing your position, it is important to allow a stock time to settle down and fall into its range for 30 to 45 minutes after the open. Do not get shaken out of a stock. The following exit rules work extremely well for stocks that are not experiencing any extreme divergences at the open. Many of your positions may produce gaps from the close to open. If this is the case, then you would use the opening price as if it is your only price and then apply the following rules.

Losers

It is imperative to recognize that the key to successful overnight trading is to limit your losses. Therefore do not hold losers for too long.

- Close out all trades down ½ of a point from entry point.
- Close out all trades which show the least possibility of follow-through.

- Use stops that are proportionate to the price and volatility of the stock.
- By 10:30 A.M., you should be closed out of most positions and have tight stops on the remaining.

You should enter the afternoon session with a clear head, unhindered by your losses. Beginning traders should be out of all positions by 12:30 P.M.

Winners

After 10:30 A.M., do not let any winning trade turn into a loser. As the day goes on, you should only be in your best positions.

- $\frac{1}{4}$ point winner or less: apply exit rules for losers.
- $\frac{3}{8}$ of a point: watch relative strength of Nasdaq 100 or pertinent index. Place $\frac{1}{4}$ of a point trailing stop. Never let a profit of $\frac{3}{8}$ of a point turn into a loss.
- $\frac{1}{2}$ to $\frac{3}{4}$ of a point: place $\frac{1}{4}$ of a point trailing stop.
- $\frac{7}{8}$ to 1 $\frac{1}{4}$ points: place $\frac{3}{8}$ of a point trailing stop.
- 1 $\frac{3}{8}$ to 2 points: place $\frac{1}{2}$ of a point trailing stop.
- 2 $\frac{3}{8}$ to 2 $\frac{3}{4}$ points: place $\frac{5}{8}$ of a point trailing stop.
- 2 $\frac{7}{8}$ to 3 $\frac{3}{4}$ points: place $\frac{3}{4}$ of a point trailing stop.
- >3 $\frac{3}{4}$ points: place 1 point trailing stop.

The following chart will illustrate the strength of your positions relative to the market. The overnight positions should be flat early in the day unless the momentum continues. Also, use the chart below to try to determine what your profit potential may be.

Symbol	Price Change +/−; Volume Change +/−	Futures— S&P 500; Nasdaq Composite	Market Rating— Dow; Nasdaq	Profit/Loss Expectation

Market momentum (price, movement up/down, volume) is a very strong indicator of the next move. How many times have you seen a takeover and checked the action for the previous day? More often than not the previous action was rising price with increasing volume. Conversely, when there is a negative announcement about a stock, it is often preceded by negative momentum.

More Tips

Here is some more information that may help you with stock selections.

- Trade only stocks with no more than $3/8$ of a point spread between the bid and offer.
- For *Over-the-Counter* (OTC) stocks, trade only stocks with at least 10 market makers.
- Getting out of position before 9:30 A.M.: not recommended on losers. Alright on winners if they are off their high or low by 1 point or more.
- Getting out into strength: not recommended unless your position is not moving with the market. Watch relative strength versus the Nasdaq 100, the S&P 500, and the Dow Jones Industrial index.
- 2-day holds: It is not advisable to take home a position for a second day unless you are up $1/2$ of a point or more after the first day.
- Hedging: You should trade long and short: 3:1 maximum long versus short, 3:1 maximum short versus long. Example: If you have $100,000 buying power, you should be hedged at $75,000. Some successful OTS traders remain market-neutral overnight. (Example: 1:1, $100,000 buying power, $50,000 long, and $50,000 short.)
- Usually the best overnight markets trade counter to their trend between 2:30 and 3:00 P.M. Do not get caught up in this move.
- Be careful of a reversal between 3:30 and 3:40 P.M. Do not panic.
- Try to hang on to your positions for the first 10 minutes each morning. You do not want to be forced out by the market in the first few minutes. If a stock you own is against you at the open,

try to give the stock ³⁄₈ to ¹⁄₂ of a point to possibly find a bottom or top.

- If a market trends abnormally strong in either direction (200 points or more swing), the odds of a follow-through the next day decrease; therefore, trading via a traditional, momentum style is unwarranted. Therefore, I recommend more hedging, fewer positions, and smaller size per position.

- Option expiration may cause the market to reverse. Therefore, I recommend more hedging, fewer positions, and smaller size per position.

- Short-term trends typically last three days; therefore, the odds of a follow-through decrease each day in markets or stocks.

Trading Routine

A.M.

1. Set up computer screen with overnight stock positions.
2. Check to see if there is any news on your stock including upgrades and downgrades.
3. Monitor stock and bond futures to gauge where the market will open.
4. Write down your sell or buy stops and limits for each position. Remember, as the price changes, so do these.

P.M.

1. Start overnight search at 2:00 P.M. and verify stocks to see if they meet these criteria.
   a. For OTC stocks—10 market makers or more
   b. No more than ³⁄₈ of a point spread
   c. Does not have earnings due within three days
   d. 5 to 10 market makers at each level
   e. At least ³⁄₄ of a point range for the day

2. Check industry groups.
    a. If a particular group is weak, stay away from buying a strong stock in that sector.
    b. Do not short a weak stock in a strong sector.
    c. If earnings are due out for an industry group leader, do not trade any stock in that sector.

3. If the book-to-bill ratio is due out, stay away from the whole sector.

4. Do not put on all positions at any one time of day (Figure 5-1).

3:00–3:15 P.M.	20% of positions
3:15–3:30 P.M.	20% of positions
3:30–3:45 P.M.	20% of positions
3:45 P.M.–close	Close out all trades reversing, replace with new positions that meet criteria and will round out overnight positions to provide the best chance for success.

Positions:

	3:00+	3:15+	3:30+	3:45+
Longs	_____	_____	_____	_____
_____	_____	_____	_____	
_____	_____	_____	_____	
Shorts	_____	_____	_____	_____
_____	_____	_____	_____	
_____	_____	_____	_____	

You can use a worksheet in the form of a quadrant chart to help gauge market and sector strength between 3 and 4 P.M. The quadrant chart simply divides the final trading hour into four 15-minute segments.

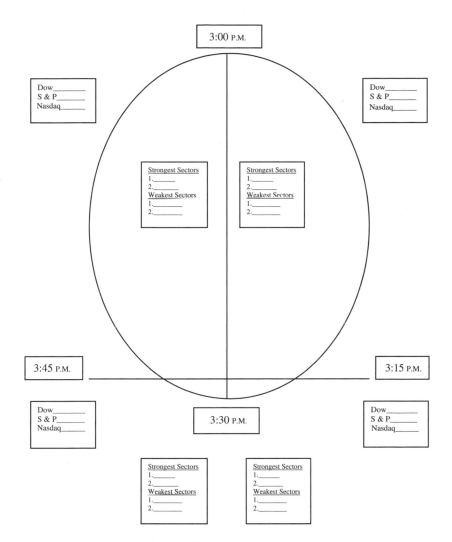

Figure 5-1. The Quadrant Chart.

CHAPTERR

A SMORGASBORD OF TRADING STRATEGIES

THE FOLLOWING IS A SMORGASBORD of strategies. Remember, you don't want to use every one, just as you don't want to eat every dish in a smorgasbord. You want to pick and choose the ones which best suit your taste, then sit down and digest them. Just remember to combine them. The more reasons you have for buying a stock, the more successful that trade is likely to be.

Range Trading

This strategy is good for both NYSE and Nasdaq stocks. Range trading is a basic strategy that all traders use to some degree.

Range trading depends on a simple fact of market life: stocks tend to bounce around in a range before they break out into a new high or low. You have a greater likelihood of succeeding with this technique once you learn how to use it properly. Just make sure that you have tight stops. How tight depends on the kind of trader you are. The smaller your time frame, the tighter your stop must be. The longer your time frame, the more room you can give a stock to go up and down. Most money managers cut their losses at 20 percent. Paul O'Neil cuts them at 8 percent. (Paul O'Neil was covered in an earlier chapter.)

There's no right answer as to when to sell. Just follow the basic principle: cut your losses, ride your gains. Beginning traders tend to do what is counterintuitive: so happy to have any profit, they'll cut their winners after a half point or so, but hang on to their losers for dear life, figuring that the stock has to turn around eventually. No, it doesn't. Sell, then buy it back when it drops further. A trader cannot be profitable with half-point winners and five-point losers.

Stripped to its essentials, here's how range trading works: buy on a pullback from a high within a stock's trading range, sell when it moves up from a low within its range. When a stock comes in to a price support area, it is considered a lower-risk purchase.

Range trading takes patience. You have to find a group of stocks, which don't all have to be in one industry, whose ups and downs you monitor for several months. That way you get to know the rhythms of these stocks, their ups and downs compared to the overall market. The idea of range trading is to buy a stock while it moves within its range.

Traders who work with NYSE stocks should stick to securities in the S&P 500. *Over-the-Counter* (OTC) traders should start with the Nasdaq 100. Day traders focus on yesterday's and today's price ranges. They are concerned with yesterday's close, high, and low, along with today's open, high, and low.

Swing traders use a five-day range. A position trader, one with a trading time frame of more than five days would consult the daily charts looking for new highs and new lows, support, and resistance, over the previous couple of months.

Range trading basically is looking for the low end of the range, using support and resistance factors. The factors could be trendlines, or highs and lows, over the last week, month, or year.

Typical range traders buy a stock when it's at the low end of the range, where the stock is near its support level (don't wait for it to go all the way to its support), then try to sell at the high end of the range. If the range trader is fortunate, the stock price will break through the top of the range and now its resistance level becomes its support level.

For example, if the stock were trading in a range between 80 and 100, and it hit 103, range traders would consider 100, which was the stock's resistance level, to now be its support level. Range traders would then hold their position and use a trailing stop at the new support level, which in this case would be 100.

However, if the stock were bought at 83 and then headed downward to 77, breaking through its support level, range traders would have to get out of that position immediately. There's no point in waiting around hoping the trade will get better. It went bad and it's time to bail out. And, of course, it follows that the broken support has now become a resistance level.

Nasdaq Industry Group Range Trading

This range trade allows for greater volatility and more room on your stops. As such, it is recommended that you trade a smaller share amount than you usually do. You must be willing to lose more points while trying to make more. Going in, you have to decide how much you're willing to lose. Say your maximum loss will be $2000. You look at charts and determine that the support is ten points. Normally, that's a lot more room than in Range Trade. If your stop is at 10 points, and you're willing to lose $2000, then you divide the two and come up with the number of shares you must buy on this trade. In this case, that's 200 shares.

Identify industry groups in a strong uptrend. Then identify individual stocks in that group that are one step below the leaders. This is geared to smaller, volatile Nasdaq stocks. It's not good for the better-known stocks such as Microsoft, Intel, or Cisco, that seem to have a life of their own. If you're trading a hot sector, don't trade the market leader. Work with the stocks that have a good chart pattern, a good run-up, have broken through resistance, but are not the large-cap stocks in that sector.

Capitalize on a countertrend in the group, or in the market, by buying a strong stock that followed the group or the market down.

Add to your position in that stock if it sells off further while the group and/or the market also is selling off. Add to your position also when the group begins to strengthen. If it does not rebound when the group and/or the market recovers, then set a stop and honor it.

Range Breakout

Range breakouts are a different kind of animal from range trading. There really are only two kinds of trades: value and momentum. Range traders buy value within a trading range. They establish that a particular stock generally trades in a certain range, such as 80 to 100. The range traders try to buy at the low end of the range and sell at the high end. They try to buy low and sell high. That's a value play.

A range breakout trade is a momentum, trend trade. Instead of buying and selling a stock as it rises and falls within a range, range breakout traders are always buying or selling a stock when it breaks through a top or bottom. Range breakout traders either look for a new 52-week high or low, or else establish a range and wait for the stock price to break through the top or bottom.

If a stock is trading between 80 and 100, the breakout trader would buy the stock after it broke through the 100 barrier. For example, if the stock trading between 80 and 100 goes to 102, then the breakout trader would buy the stock with a trailing stop at 100, which is now considered the stock's support level.

If that same stock broke down below 80, to 78, a breakout trader would short the stock. If the stock keeps going down, then the breakout trader sticks with it. If the stock rises and breaks 80, which is now its new resistance level, then the trader would buy back the stock and dissolve the trade. Because this technique is a momentum method, it is biased toward hot-sector Nasdaq stocks.

Growth Stock Breakout

This strategy lets you buy a growth stock when it breaks into a new 52-week high. Before you hit that buy button, though, check

Investor's Business Daily to make sure the stock meets the following qualifications:

1. Current quarterly earnings per share are up at least 30 percent from the previous quarter.
2. Sales growth of at least four quarters.
3. 80–80: The stock must be in a strong industry group where at least 80 percent of the stocks are rising in price. The stock's price must be higher than 80 percent of the companies in its industry group (relative strength rating).
4. Over the previous few weeks, as the stock rises, there should be consistent buying of the stock in blocks of 10,000 shares or more. That shows that the stock has strong institutional sponsorship or mutual fund interest.
5. The stock price must be near a 52-week high, poised for a breakout.

Relative Strength

You've already learned something about this technique and you know it can be used in many ways and in many forms. It's especially important for momentum traders. Now here's a refinement, which is good for both NYSE and Nasdaq stocks: look for strength plus higher-than-average volume. Why? If you have a combination of strong prices and strong demand, you have a very powerful sign that the stock will move well in the future. Basically, you're trying to find out three different facts:

1. Is your stock strong or weak compared to other stocks in its industry group?
2. Is your stock strong or weak compared to the market as a whole?
3. Is your stock price strong or weak compared to its usual trading range?

When you're using relative strength, you are buying stocks which are strong and shorting stocks which are down. That's the absolute rule. The hard part is figuring out where you will get in and where you will get out. If your stock is strong, meaning that for whatever period you are trading the stock is up, and the market is weak (heading downward), that tells you that when the market comes back, your stock will do well, too.

Buy quality stocks over $20. You're a lot better off buying strong stocks in a strong industry group. Don't buy a cheap stock in a strong industry group assuming that the stock will get a lot stronger. That's not likely to happen. Strong is strong for a reason.

The idea is to buy when a stock drops temporarily and sell it short when it rises temporarily. But to execute that strategy, here are some specific rules:

1. The most basic rule when trading off of relative strength is the one you have to follow the most religiously: don't buy a down stock or short an up stock—ever. You'll be tempted to violate this rule. Don't. You'll save yourself a lot of money.

2. Always wait for a definitive rise or fall in the market.

3. If the market makes a move up, start looking for the weakest stocks for the time period you're trading. Wait for a bounce, then start building your short position. When the market starts to rally, short stocks which have been down the lowest for the day, or short weak stocks which are in a weak industry group. This is called shorting on the bounce.

4. If the market makes a move down and you see a trend, focus on the stocks which are up for the day. Pick one of the stocks which is up the most for the day or a strong stock in a strong industry group. When the price drops, start buying, expecting the price to go up. This method is called buying on a pullback, which you've heard about before.

5. If the market is strongly up or down, then you have to be more careful. When the market is at extremes, it's better to just trade where the trend is. Don't try to buy stocks when the market is down a lot, because they likely will have trouble bouncing back. If the market is up a lot, don't sell short, because the market is moving too powerfully in an up trajectory. On most days, though, it's safe to trade in both directions.

6. If you are a swing trader, it is important to gauge the strength of the overall market based on the major indices. If there is a major divergence between them, trade with the strength.

7. Pick stocks in hot industries. In a market that's going up, you surely wouldn't want to start trading in an industry group where the price of the top stock is creeping along below the market average. In the later 1990s, for example, industries which gained a lot of ground included technology, banking, and brokerages. Trade only within the top 10 industries, as measured by *Investor's Business Daily.*

Resume Trend

Stocks that closed strongly yesterday sometimes open lower today, and weak closers sometimes open higher. Then, a bit later, yesterday's trend will emerge again—the apparent change in trends turned out to be merely pauses before a trend continued. You need patience to identify such reversals. Wait for stocks that closed at their highs and opened lower to resume their upward movement past yesterday's close. Then buy $1/8$ above the close.

For stocks that closed at their low and opened higher, take the same approach: wait for them to resume their downward drift past yesterday's close. Then sell short $1/8$ below the close.

On March 1, 2000, Lucent (LU) closed at 68 $5/8$ (up 9 $1/8$ for the day). The following day, LU opened at 68, then traded lower, then resumed a trend above 68 $5/8$ and closed at 71 $3/4$.

Low-Volume Resume Trend

Vic Salamone, principal of On-Site Trading, Inc., Hackensack, New Jersey, uses this technique with great success. The approach is more technical than Resume Trend and works best for listed stocks which have a low volume, generally less than 200,000 shares per day.

To use this technique, focus on stocks which, at the end of the day, have made a low which is equal to or lower than the day before, and then have finished the day with a gain. In addition, the stock must have had volume larger than the previous day's and was in an uptrend higher than the 50-day moving average.

You can give secondary consideration to listed stocks which are below their 50-day moving average, but which are still above the 150- or 200-day moving average, with volume in a strong uptrend.

That strong volume is a signal that it's still a good time to buy the stock. Avoid stocks with weak money flow patterns. Stocks which actually hit their moving average, whether it's a 20-, 50-, 150-, or 200-day moving average, without breaking through it, also are good candidates. Look for strong signs that the stock price is moving up. When the price of these stocks drop, that's usually a normal pullback. Pullbacks to a support are also good.

If a stock qualifies for consideration, place a buy stop above the previous day's high. If the stock opens unchanged or below where it finished the day before, then goes above the previous day's high, let the order stand. If the stock opens higher than the previous day's close or if the stock makes a lower low than the previous day, cancel the trade.

The theory behind this strategy is simply that an opening weaker than the previous day's close usually chases people away from the stock, and that's a common bit of Wall Street warfare which happens before a stock's price advances. By not buying a strong opening, you won't end up chasing a stock which starts out strong, then fizzles out and heads downward, leaving you as the unwitting buyer with a loss. Of course there will be stocks which start out strong and stay strong, but by not buying a strong opening, you cut the number of possible losing trades.

If you wait to buy until the stock price goes above yesterday's high, you're buying on strength, not weakness, and momentum is on your side. You avoid the most common trading error: buying on weakness, hoping for a bounce or rally—only to see the stock continue to go lower. The trader who habitually buys on weakness will end up with more losers than winners. The stock probably is down for a reason. Remember, there will be plenty of stocks which go up from a lower point.

Here's how to set your stop loss and reentry points for this technique:

1. Use a $1/4$ to $3/8$ point stop loss. This tight stop will keep your losses in check. Using this stop-loss point usually works right from the get-go. A stock which pulls back $3/8$ from your point of entry has a high probability of having already topped out for the day, and is even more likely to meander or go lower.

2. However, if your stop loss has been executed and you've taken a loss, and the stock goes either no lower or $1/8$ of a point lower than your stop loss (but a maximum of $1/2$ point from your entry)

and then starts to rally on strong volume, reenter trade at your previous buy point. For example, suppose you've bought a stock at 70, using this strategy, and you've executed a stop loss when the price slipped to 69 $^5/_8$. If the stock slips down to 69 $^1/_2$, then starts back up on strong volume, you would want to place a buy order to be executed at 70.

This approach takes into account that a shakeout has happened, and now the stock is moving back up. Use this strategy, though, only if the stock went no higher than your buy price before slipping downward, executing your stop loss. If the stock went higher than your buy price by $^1/_8$ or more, and then pulled back to trigger your stop loss order, don't buy back in. You could end up being whipsawed as the price stops out, then rises, then falls, then rises, then falls. Go on to the next trade instead.

Please note: once you've made a profit on a stock using this strategy, don't buy back in. Go on to another stock with a new signal. If you buy back the stock after you've snagged a profit, you're now day-trading, and your odds of making a profit are lower. Try to stay in a trade as long as you can. If the stock makes a quick one-point gain, sell at least half your holding. If the stock is up $^1/_8$ or $^1/_4$ of a point, either sell half your position to reduce your risk or sell all your position and get out. There will always be another trade. Use breakeven stops, which are set for your entry point, for any position which moves up $^3/_8$ from where you bought it. At least you won't lose money that way.

Oversold, Overbought

This tool will be used only in special situations, when a listed or Nasdaq market cap stock is hit extraordinarily hard as a result of either bad news, bad earnings results, or an analyst's downgrade. The strategy employed by buying these stocks is known as bottom fishing, in the hope that the stock was driven too low and should rebound. The risk involved, compared to the possible reward, should be strongly in our favor.

Conversely, stocks that appear to be overbought should generally be avoided until a top is identified. Wait until the stock shows a definitive reversal of its trend. Missing the first one or two percent of the move downward may be for the best.

When buying oversold stocks, you may have to go fishing a few times, employ tight stops, and be willing to lose only a little, a few times, before you are right. When you are right, let your profits run.

Fading the Opening

This technique is useful only for NYSE stocks and works best for nonvolatile S&P stocks. It takes advantage of the fact that the specialists are required to keep an orderly market; if there are significantly more buy than sell orders, or vice versa, at the opening, they have to address the problem. Sometimes that means spending their own money, and they want to make sure they profit when they do. Here's how to figure out when to use this technique: for the NYSE, the openings for stocks are staggered. If a stock opening will be delayed past 9:40 A.M., the specialists must publish at what price they think the stock will open. The report usually reads something like, "IBM Indication 102–105." If there's a change in the expected opening, specialists must report that fact. Scan your news service for indications, looking for large gaps. Almost any good news service will tell you this information. The more extreme the news— earnings, warnings, takeovers, and the resulting gap—the better. Place your order before the open as a premarket open order. Such orders generally must be entered ten minutes before the opening of the stock to be guaranteed the opening price.

The further down a stock opens, the more likely it is that the specialists are spending their own money, because they're offering such a bargain price to buyers. That's a good time for you to snap up the bargain. If the stock opens, say, 10 points down, you can be sure the specialists will be trying to push the stock price higher in order to sell their own shares and profit from buying so low. In this case, when they profit, you profit. Keep tight stops. The same principle applies in reverse to shorting an extreme gap up.

On October 19, 2000, the market opened sharply lower led downward by three stocks. By fading the open on these three listed stocks, you could have capitalized on the oversold condition.

International Business Machines (IBM), closed at 113, opened at 90.25 at 9:46, traded as high as 96 at 9:57.

J.P.Morgan (JPM), closed at 137.625, opened at 118 at 9:45, traded as high as 120 at 9:58 and as high as 122 at 10:06.

EMC Corporation (EMC), closed at 94.938, opened at 86 at 9:51, traded as high as 88.5 at 9:57 and as high as 90 at 9:59.

Tip: Look closely at the stock's actual opening and compare it to the range the specialist indicated for the opening. Suppose the specialist says the stock should open between 55 and 58. If the stock opens near the bottom of the range, that's a good sign if you want to sell. For example, if the stock closed at 50 the night before, then opens at 55, that means the buy imbalance has been met and the initial enthusiasm may not be as great as anticipated.

Similarly, if the specialist's indication said the stock would open at 55–58, and a few moments later the indication dropped to 52–55, then the initial wave of buying has been met and the specialist needs more buyers. This may also be a good time to short the open.

However, if the specialist's indications in the morning before the opening are constantly being revised upward as the opening draws nearer and nearer, and then the price opens at the top of the indicated range, don't fade the open. Instead, see how it trades.

Buying a Gap Opening

As you probably remember, a gap opening happens when a stock jumps higher or lower than it closed the day before. To buy a gap opening, make sure the stock gaps open at least a point for listed stocks and at least two points for Nasdaq issues.

First, let the stock trade for a minimum of a half hour. After that, put a buy stop in at $1/8$–$1/4$ above the highest price of the first 30 minutes. At the same time put in a sell stop order at $1/8$–$1/4$ below the lowest price so far for that entire day. Look for a $1.50–$2 a share advance, usually within a few hours.

In addition, the larger the gap, the better off you are, especially if the gap opened up because of some terrific news such as a large contract, a merger, or great earnings.

Through the Opening

While we generally don't favor rigid patterns, this one is simple and quite useful. It results from a stock opening down, then quickly doing a 180 and going back up.

Remember, use this approach only on stocks of large, well-known companies that are included in most trading programs and have a daily range of at least two points. These are companies which are so strong they're not likely to sell off very much, so any dip will be seen as a buying opportunity and people will rush in to buy it.

For a trade to work on this technique, the stock has to open, then sell off at least one-third of its daily range, or at least $3/8$. Then the stock wheels around and the price heads back to above the opening. Combine "Through the Opening" with "Buying a Gap Opening" or fundamental analysis, such as a breaking news story, if you can. Remember, the more reasons to do the trade the better.

To use this technique, make sure you buy within the first 30 minutes of trading and use very tight stops. The greater the sell-off and the quicker the stock price comes back through the open, the better. The open is the key support resistance point of the first hour of trading. This technique, in combination with news, can be used in reverse for short sales.

Key Reversal

This is another pattern technique which, like "Through the Open," is especially useful. You can use it for one particular stock or for the NYSE and Nasdaq markets as a whole. Key reversal happens fast, a one-day wonder in which a stock's price starts out higher than the high of the day before, or lower than the low of the day before, keeps that trend for a while, then reverses on high volume and closes the day strongly, having gone in exactly the opposite direction of the morning trend. You want to buy or sell the closing reversal trend.

This strategy works best for buying reversal bottoms and selling reversal tops. Put stop orders slightly above the new highs or lows made on that key reversal day.

Sympathy Trades

This technique might well be named "The Tagalong Method," and it's good for both exchanges. Basically, it's this: stocks in any industry group often will head in the same direction as one stock which is standing out, for whatever reason. If a disk maker reports bad earnings, then traders would consider other disk makers likely to be in the same boat and would begin selling off their holdings in all disk-making companies. That's a good time to short.

If a disk maker announces it's being bought, then traders think that other disk makers might merge, too. Traders rush in to buy and the stock prices of similar companies go up in sympathy.

This method also works particularly well if a stock is way up on no news. Other stocks in its industry which are not yet up in sympathy will trade in accordance. For example, on February 10, 2000, Satyam Infoway (SIFY), a provider of Internet services in India, gained 16 points on no news. Icici Limited (IC), a virtual bank in India, failed to make a move on February 10, but gained nine points in the next two days.

Percent Volume Gainers

If a stock's volume has a huge jump in percentage and there's been no news at all, watch that stock carefully, whether it's on the NYSE or Nasdaq. Usually this event is a sign that insiders are buying heavily, and the stock could make a big move soon.

Buying Prints

This technique, good only for NYSE stocks, has to do with supply and demand. Anytime there's been a sale of 100,000 or more shares (called prints), which usually is done at one point less than the market, put in a buy order immediately. Why? Because it's highly likely that the available supply has been exhausted, and the specialist will have to offer a higher price to get more sellers.

When a specialist spreads a stock quote by a point or more, many traders will try to buy on the bid or sell on the offer in anticipation of quick reversals after the print. This technique works best when the stock is making a new day's high or low. Set a tight stop. Look for this to occur when a stock is way up or down for the day. Be wary of extremely volatile stocks.

Pre- or Postmarket Trend

Some traders will buy and sell shares after hours on the Electronic Communications Networks such as Instinet, Island, and REDI. If you decide you want to do after-hours trading, here are some guidelines:

1. Always go with the trend.
2. Get in on a trade shortly after news is announced, otherwise you may get whipsawed.
3. Get out if your position goes against you.
4. If your position is a winner, get out of at least half of the position at the next day's open. You can always buy back more.
5. Limit yourself to extremes in the news, good or bad—such as earnings reports, earnings preannouncements, takeover announcements, mergers, or strategic alliances—to assure that you'll be following a definite trend and that there will be enough interest to assure liquidity.
6. As soon as the news is announced, look for possible crossed-market arbitrage opportunities on Instinet, REDI, and Island.

If you have access to more than one after-hours system, you can beat the institutions here. That's because many institutions use only Instinet, and they won't know what's happening on the other systems. Sometimes news comes out, such as Microsoft announcing a stock split. The stock price starts trading up. Instinet might show someone bidding for Microsoft at 110, while REDI might show someone selling Microsoft at 109 1/2. A trader with quick fingers would buy the offer on REDI at 109 1/2 and sell the offer on Instinet at 110 for a half-point profit taking only seconds to execute.

Selling Short

You must learn to short both Nasdaq and NYSE stocks. However, you're probably better off as a beginner selling Nasdaq stocks short only for day trading. Nasdaq stocks are too volatile, and too many things can go wrong, to short for any longer than one day. Just remember: the big plus to short selling is that downward moves generally are faster and larger than upward moves.

The best reason to know how to sell short is so you will have a balanced trading attack. You will know how to participate in bull and bear markets. Many traders profit more from their short sales. You need to have as many trading techniques as possible at your command, and selling short is one of the most fundamental.

In short selling, pick stocks with high P-E ratios. They're the most vulnerable if bad news hits. The best bets are stocks with P-E ratios of 75 or more. The really plump targets are the ones whose P-Es are at least 50 percent higher than either the rest of the market or their own industry group. Avoid shorting stocks which have been down several days in a row on major volume. An exhausted sell-off could reverse. Stocks which retrace more than 50 percent from their highs are also good short candidates.

Hedges

A *hedge* is a stock purchase or short sale that reduces the risk of other equity positions. *You must follow this rule for hedges:* Once you start holding positions overnight, you must keep your long trades and your short trades at a 3:1 ratio. If you have committed $75,000 in long trades, then you must commit $25,000 in short ones, or vice versa. Over the course of time, this ratio will help bail you out on more occasions than you can imagine. Essentially, by using this ratio, you have a permanent backup plan in case the market goes against you.

Hedges are essential tools if you're going to sell short, because short-selling a single stock can be risky for swing traders. That's why many traders use index-based hedges. If you're putting money into an index, you're investing in 30, 100, or even thousands of companies all at once, and when you do, you're betting that their specific index will go down. This method is the safest way to short stocks. It's a whole lot better than shorting just one stock.

One of the big pluses to an index hedge is that it looks like a mutual fund, yet you can trade it like a stock. As long as there's an exchange open somewhere, you can buy or sell all your indexed shares whenever you like, unlike a mutual fund, which can be cashed in only at the close of the trading day. Sometimes you'll even be paid dividends. An added bonus: because they are indexes, they're meant to mimic a specific collection of stocks, which means the index will already own the shares of the stocks the index is trying to replicate. That means very little stock trading, which in turn means not a lot of capital gains distributions, which you'd have to factor into your taxes.

Index hedges are a conservative money management technique which will serve you well in the long run. There are several indices, all traded on the *American Stock Exchange* (AMEX), which you may want to consider. First, however, know the basic rule for index shorting: short the sectors in which you also have a long position. Remember, hedging is supposed to balance out your other positions, so make sure you're shorting the same sectors in which you are long. Here are the indices:

- **Spiders. (Actually, it's SPDR, short for Standard & Poor's Depository Receipts.)** It's based on the entire S&P 500 Composite Stocks, largely on the NYSE. It's traded under the designation "SPY." Its creators say that selling SPDR shares won't result in any taxes. If you're taking long positions in NYSE stocks, then this index is the one you should be shorting.

- **Nasdaq-100 Shares.** Traded under the "QQQ" symbol. This index is a list of the most capitalized companies in the Nasdaq exchange. If you're buying Nasdaq stocks long, then this index is the one you should be shorting.

- **Diamonds.** Traded under the "DIA" symbol, this is an index of the stocks in the Dow Jones Industrial Average. If you're buying DJIA stocks long, then this index is the one you should be shorting.

- **Midcap Spiders.** Similar to SPDRs, but this one includes the S&P Midcap 400 stocks. It trades under the "MDY" symbol.

- **Sector Spiders.** There are also SPDRs for various sectors within the Standard & Poor's 500. There are nine of them. Two are in the consumer group: the Consumer Services Sector (XLV) and the

Consumer Staples Sector (XLP). The others are Basic Industries Sector (XLB), Cyclicals/Transportation Sector (XLY), Energy Sector (XLE), Financial Sector (XLF), Industrial Sector (XLI), Technology Sector (XLK), and the Utilities Sector (XLU).

Position Trading

As you probably remember from earlier in the chapter, position trading is for traders who will hold a stock for at least five days, and perhaps even many months. As a position trader, you should be trying to find ways to have a diversified portfolio of stocks, because having that portfolio will help your holdings stand up over the length of time that you're keeping the securities. The longer you hold stocks, the more you need a diversified portfolio to minimize your risk.

As a position trader, you might choose a stock on the basis of earnings expectations, increased volume, a stock split announcement, outstanding performance, or an excellent chart pattern suggesting a possible momentum breakout. The stock must have a substantial profit potential to justify the greater risk (because you're holding it longer than usual) of the price heading downward.

As a position trader, you've got to diversify over a large sampling of trades across and within market sectors to get more true diversity. If you're long 10 stocks, but they're all oil drillers, that's better than being long one oil driller, but that's not real diversity. It's a lot more effective when you spread your risk around by taking several positions, spreading the risk among several different parts of the market.

In the small stock sector, you should be looking for stocks which are positioned well: they've got a lock or near-lock on their industry and aren't too affected by whatever stage the economic cycle is in; they can be expanded to new regions without much trouble and have a lot of repeat orders because the product is disposable. The company should be doing well financially: earnings should be climbing at least 25 percent a year and earnings per share by 30 percent.

William J. O'Neil, in his *24 Essential Lessons for Investment Success*, uses several guidelines, including fundamental, technical, and timing issues. He says that you need all of them to pick a truly superior stock, one that's ahead of the pack in its industry and has little or, even better, no competition.

His first screen focuses on fundamental questions. He wants to make sure the stock costs between $16 and $150 for Nasdaq stocks and between $20 and $75 for NYSE securities. Good stocks cost good money. Don't try to buy the cheapest stock in a sector and figure it will climb with the rest of its group. That won't happen.

O'Neil looks for an upward direction in the market generally, and sales growth (6 to 12 quarters, accelerating in recent quarters). Earnings are extremely important: they should be higher than expected in the most recent quarters, up at least 25 percent, and estimates for the next quarter's earnings should be up by a decent amount.

He also has earnings criteria for growth stocks (earnings up at least 25 percent each year for three years; an earnings-per-share rating of 80 or higher, according to *Investor's Business Daily;* and turnarounds (at least two quarters of strong earnings, the trailing 12-month earnings near the peak of the past couple of years, and strong consensus earnings estimates for the next two years).

Taxes matter, too. The company must have a minimum 18 percent pretax margin (lower for retailers), and a current after-tax profit margin near the company's peak. Both pretax and after-tax margins should be improving over many quarters, and those margins should be among the industry's best. In addition, the company should have at least 20 percent return on equity.

Going with the trend is also vital: O'Neil advocates finding stocks that are in a sector that historically does well, whose capitalization the market currently favors, and is in a part of the economy (cyclical, defensive, new stocks or old, and so on) whose stocks are currently doing well.

Then there are issues about the company itself: the management should own the stock, the backlog of unfilled orders should be growing (know at what capacity the company is operating and the expected rate of future expansion), and you should really know and understand what the company's business is and believe in it strongly.

Then there are the technical analysis questions, of which there are a lot fewer. The company should have an Investor's Business Daily Relative Price Strength Rating of at least 80. Check to see if professional buyers are accumulating the stock. If they are, maybe you should be, too. In addition, the stock should have a minimum 50 percent volume increase on the day you start buying it.

The following strategies are pegged to news events.

Stock Splits

Stock splits are big news. When companies split shares, they are giving the stockholder more shares (giving stockholders a 2-for-1 split, meaning they now will have twice as many shares as before) or fewer shares than they currently have (1-for-2 split would mean that shareholders now have half the stock they had before). The stock's price changes proportionately on the day the split is executed.

More commonly by far, the company gives more shares rather than fewer. By giving stockholders more shares, the price is lowered and the stock is more affordable and accessible to more investors. This kind of split happens when a company is optimistic about its future. There's reason to be optimistic about the future of a stock after it's been split so that shareholders will have more shares than they had before. Paul Cherney of "RightLine Power Trading" has analyzed the effects of stock splits and found that, on average, stock splits outperform nonsplits by more than 8 percent for the year following the split, rise 4.35 percent for the 20 days before the split, and 4.59 percent in the 20 days after the split. In addition, on average, the effects of the split materialize in the 30 days surrounding the day the split actually takes place.

Day traders, note: if an announcement of a stock split occurs during the trading day, jump on it. The stock price is likely to move up, if only for a little while. That's not always true, but as a rule, that's what happens.

Quiet Period Ends

The SEC bans companies from promoting themselves and hyping their stock for 40 to 90 days around the time a new issue of stock is put on the market. That time is called the quiet period. For *Initial Public Offerings* (IPOs), the quiet period ends 25 days after the day the IPO is first put on the market. For IPOs there also is no analyst coverage for that period.

When that 25-day period for IPOs ends, then analysts start covering the stock with buy ratings and the company starts pouring out press releases, both of which can give a boost to the stock's price.

Beware, though. As more people learn about this phenomenon, the price pop is happening more frequently just before the period ends.

Lockup Expires

Lockups are periods of time, usually 180 days, during which insiders—that usually includes board members and the most senior executives—are barred from selling their shares after an IPO. After that period, a lot of shares might be dumped on the market if those executives sell, and the price could drop substantially. Because a number of traders are familiar with this fact, they now are selling their shares a few days to a few weeks before the lockup ends.

However, that fear of a drop in the price is also grounded in reality. Two Penn State University finance professors, Gordon Hanka and Laura Field, studied what happens when lockup agreements expire. They studied 3127 IPOs, and discovered that the end of a lockup can be a bad time for investors. The study found that, on average, a stock's price drops 1.8 percent when the lockup ends. The drop also does not bounce back on its own. The price will go up only on the basis of good news. Recently the price drops have been even worse. They've averaged about 2.5 percent between 1994 and 1996.

A price drop, combined with increased trading when a lockup period ends, is even more pronounced, the professors found, with companies backed by venture funds. That's because venture funds are far more aggressive sellers than other shareholders, probably so they can nail down their profits.

If you're going to invest in a company which has newly gone public, here are some tips:

- Find out when the lockup expires.
- Watch out for IPOs six months after they went public. Sell before the six months are up, instead of waiting for that seventh month.
- Don't buy the stock during the 2 to 3 weeks just before the lockup period ends.

For some companies, the demand is so strong that when the lockup period ends, the stock price actually goes up. Remember, stocks don't automatically go down just because a lockup or quiet period ends. It's important for you to find out what percentage of the float is being released. Usually, perhaps 20 percent of the shares are sold at the IPO, so the insiders still own a lot of the stock. Look at the whole picture first. One place to find more information on lockup period expirations, including how much stock can be released, is ipolockup.com

Of course, it's extremely rare for all the shares that *could* be sold after the lockup ends to actually *be* sold. Nonetheless, the fear of the IPO's price going down after the lockup ends is real, and it does affect the market. Many traders actually view a significant drop in price as a buying opportunity.

The Index Effect

This technique focuses on the Standard & Poor's 500 (S&P 500), which in fact does have exactly 500 stocks in it. It's an important index because it's a widely used standard for judging how well or poorly money managers have fared. The stocks for the index are picked by the Standard & Poor's Index Committee because they are leading companies which are at or near the top of leading industries. The S&P 500 is also supposed to be a reflection of the whole U.S. stock market. When added together, the capitalization of the S&P 500 stocks totals about $7 billion.

When a company becomes listed as one of the S&P 500, that's considered a momentous event—price jumps of between 3 and 6 percent during the days following the evening announcement are not unusual. It's not quite like a football player or a baseball player making it into their respective halls of fame, but it's close. Even Internet stocks are now making the list—Yahoo recently was added, the first Internet company to be included.

To be considered for entry into the S&P 500, a company's *float*, the number of shares owned by the public, is supposed to be at least half of the entire stock. Many Internet, and other, stocks are still largely in the hands of the company founders and principals. For the guidelines, check out S&P's Web site at www.spyglobal.com.

Trying to figure out which companies will be the next ones chosen for the S&P 500 has become serious business on Wall Street. Many traders, money managers, and hedge funds try to predict which stocks are most likely to be picked and then buy shares in those stocks. They look at a company's float and for leading companies which are at or near the top of leading industries. Another approach would be to buy the largest stocks in the S&P 400 Midcap Index. Those companies have a pretty good chance of being picked.

Insider Trading

Insider trading, if done correctly, is perfectly legal. Anyone who is part of a company's management or board of directors can sell or buy shares, but they have to publicly report it within 10 days after the end of the month in which they've done it. What insiders do with the stock of their own company can be used as a fundamental indicator. However, whoever is buying or selling could be in error about the company's prospects. Nonetheless, insider trading certainly is of interest to the trader. You'll probably be more interested in buying than in selling. Executives or board members would buy shares only because they expect that it will make them money, while there's no telling why someone is selling shares.

Especially watch the transactions which involve either a large number of shares or a large amount of money, particularly when done by the very top management. If more than one of them is buying, that shows a more solid consensus about the company's prospects, especially if the shares are bought on the open market. Stock options are intended to be an easy way to make money as an incentive, and cashing those in may be nothing more than prudent money management.

7

LEVEL II DAY TRADE

D AY TRADING CAN BE A SUCCESSFUL STRATEGY when a trader wants to minimize exposure to the market. Day traders spend much more time than swing traders analyzing each trade and reading the momentum changes on their screens. Their positions are opened and closed the same day. Therefore the trader must be fiercely on top of his positions and cannot afford to let a trade run as long as a swing trader. The day trader's wins on individual trades are mostly $1/8$ and $1/4$ point, with the occasional windfall of $1/2$ point or more. Consequently, losses must be cut immediately at $1/8$. Trailing stops should be employed by generally raising your stop $1/8$ of a point for every move up of $3/8$ of a point. Typically, a large number of trades are executed daily (25 to 30 or more). Because traders are in and out of so many different trades so quickly, they require less capital than the overnight or swing traders in order to turn over their money.

The following flow charts summarize the Key Level II price moments and market maker actions. It should help you anticipate price change and gauge market momentum.

Level II Momentum

Upward Momentum

Best Bid Has Axe

(particularly Institutional Firms, such as, Goldman Sachs-GSCO, Morgan Stanley-MSCO, Salomon Smith Barney-SBSH, Lehman Brothers-LEHM)

> **Goldman - The Axe is at the Best Bid**

BID			ASK		
GSCO	102 1/16	10	ISLD	102 3/16	10
REDI	102 1/16	22	INCA	102 3/16	2
SBSH	102 1/16	10	DKNY	102 3/16	5
INCA	102 1/16	16	GSCO	102 1/4	1
BTRD	102 1/16	10	SHWD	102 1/4	10
RSSF	102	10	FBCO	102 1/4	10
MONT	102	10	MWSE	102 1/4	1
PWJC	101 15/16	10	KCMO	102 1/4	10
DKNY	101 15/16	1	SLKC	102 1/4	1
BRUT	101 7/8	5			

Downward Momentum

Lowest Offer Has Axe

(particularly Institutional Firms, such as, Goldman Sachs-GSCO, Morgan Stanley-MSCO, Salomon Smith Barney-SBSH, Lehman Brothers-LEHM)

> **Goldman - The Axe is at the Lowest Offer**

BID			ASK		
REDI	102 1/16	10	GSCO	102 3/16	10
SBSH	102 1/16	XX	REDI	102 3/16	10
INCA	102 1/16	16	ISLD	102 3/16	2
BTRD	102 1/16	10	INCA	102 3/16	5
RSSF	102	10	DKNY	102 3/16	1
MONT	102	10	SHWD	102 1/4	10
PWJC	101 15/16	10	FBCO	102 1/4	1
PRU	101 15/16	1	MWSE	102 1/4	10
DKNY	101 15/16	1	KCMO	102 1/4	10
BRUT	101 7/8	5	SLKC	102 1/4	1

continues

Level II Momentum *(continued)*

Upward Momentum

Market Maker Creates Best Bid

BID

REDI	102 1/16	22
GSCO	102 1/16	10
SBSH	102 1/16	10
INCA	102 1/16	16
BTRD	102 1/16	10
RSSF	102	10
MONT	102	10
PWJC	101 15/16	10
DKNY	101 15/16	1
BRUT	101 7/8	5

ASK

REDI	102 3/16	10
← 1. Goldman @ 102 1/16	102 1/16	2
INCA	102 3/16	5
DKNY	102 3/16	1
GSCO	102 1/4	10
SHWD	102 1/4	10
FBCO	102 1/4	1
MWSE	102 1/4	10
KCMO	102 1/4	10
SLKC	102 1/4	1

Downward Momentum

Market Maker Creates Lowest Offer

BID

REDI	102 1/16	22
SBSH	10	
INCA	102 1/16	16
BTRD	102 1/16	10
RSSF	102	10
MONT	102	10
PWJC	101 15/16	10
PRUS	101 15/16	1
DKNY	101 15/16	1
BRUT	101 7/8	5

ASK

REDI	102 3/16	10
← 1. Goldman @ 102 3/16 — GSCO	102 3/16	10
ISLD	102 3/16	2
INCA	102 3/16	5
DKNY	102 3/16	1
SHWD	102 1/4	10
FBCO	102 1/4	1
MWSE	102 1/4	10
KCMO	102 1/4	10
SLKC	102 1/4	1

Market Maker Creates Best Bid

BID			ASK		
GSCO	102 1/8	10	2. Market Maker Creates Best Bid		
REDI	102 1/16	22	ISLD	102 3/16	2
SBSH	102 1/16	10	INCA	102 3/16	5
INCA	102 1/16	16	DKNY	102 3/16	1
BTRD	102 1/16	10	GSCO	102 1/4	10
RSSF	102	10	SHWD	102 1/4	10
MONT	102	10	FBCO	102 1/4	1
PWJC	101 15/16	10	MWSE	102 1/4	10
DKNY	101 15/16	1	KCMO	102 1/4	10
BRUT	101 7/8	5	SLKC	102 1/4	1

Market Maker Creates Lowest Offer

BID			ASK		
RE 2. Market Maker Creates Lowest Offer			GSCO	102 1/8	10
SBSH	102 1/16	10	REDI	102 3/16	10
INCA	102 1/16	16	ISLD	102 3/16	2
BTRD	102 1/16	10	INCA	102 3/16	5
RSSF	102	10	DKNY	102 3/16	1
MONT	102	10	SHWD	102 1/4	10
PWJC	101 15/16	10	FBCO	102 1/4	1
PRUS	101 15/16	1	MWSE	102 1/4	10
DKNY	101 15/16	1	KCMO	102 1/4	10
BRUT	101 7/8	5	SLKC	102 1/4	1

continues

Level II Momentum (continued)

Upward Momentum

Market Maker Joins Best Bid

BID			ASK		
REDI	102 1/16	22	REDI	102 3/16	10
SBSH	102 1/16	10	ISLD	102 3/16	2
INCA	102 1/16	16	INCA	102 3/16	5
BTRD	102 1/16	10	DKNY	102 3/16	1
RSSF	102	10	GSCO	102 1/4	10
GSCO	101 15/16	10	FBCO	102 1/4	1
MONT	101 15/16	10	MWSE	102 1/4	10
PWJC	101 15/16	10	KCMO	102 1/4	10
DKNY	101 15/16	1	SLKC	102 1/4	1
BRUT	101 7/8	5			

1. Goldman @ 101 15/16 → GSCO

Downward Momentum

Market Maker Joins Lowest Offer

BID			ASK		
REDI	102 1/16	22	REDI	102 3/16	10
SBSH	102 1/16	10	ISLD	102 3/16	2
INCA	102 1/16	16	INCA	102 3/16	5
BTRD	102 1/16	10	DKNY	102 3/16	1
RSSF	102	10	GSCO	102 1/4	10
MONT	102	10	SHWD	102 1/4	10
PWJC	101 15/16	10	FBCO	102 1/4	1
PRUS	101 15/16	1	MWSE	102 1/4	10
DKNY	101 15/16	1	KCMO	102 1/4	10
BRUT	101 7/8	5	SLKC	102 1/4	1

1. Goldman @ 102 1/4 → GSCO

Market Maker Joins Best Bid

BID			ASK		
REDI	102 1/16	22	REDI	102 3/16	10
GSCO	102 1/16	10	*2. Market Maker Joins Best Bid*		
SBSH	102 1/16	10	INCA	102 3/16	5
INCA	102 1/16	16	DKNY	102 3/16	1
BTRD	102 1/16	10	GSCO	102 1/4	10
RSSF	102	10	SHWD	102 1/4	10
MONT	101 15/16	10	FBCO	102 1/4	10
PWJC	101 15/16	10	MWSE	102 1/4	10
DKNY	101 15/16	1	KCMO	102 1/4	10
BRUT	101 7/8	5	SLKC	102 1/4	1

Market Maker Joins Lowest Offer

BID			ASK		
REDI	102 1/16	22	REDI	102 3/16	10
SB	*2. Market Maker Joins Lowest Offer*		GSCO	102 3/16	10
INCA	102 1/16	16	ISLD	102 3/16	2
BTRD	102 1/16	10	INCA	102 3/16	5
RSSF	102	10	DKNY	102 3/16	1
MONT	102	10	SHWD	102 1/4	10
PWJC	101 15/16	10	FBCO	102 1/4	1
PRUS	101 15/16	1	MWSE	102 1/4	10
DKNY	101 15/16	1	KCMO	102 1/4	10
BRUT	101 7/8	5	SLKC	102 1/4	1

continues

Level II Momentum (continued)

Upward Momentum

Market Maker Leaves Lowest Offer

BID			ASK		
REDI	$102\,^{1}/_{16}$	22	REDI	$102\,^{3}/_{16}$	10
SBSH	1. Goldman @ $102\,^{3}/_{16}$		GSCO ←	$102\,^{3}/_{16}$	10
INCA	$102\,^{1}/_{16}$	16	ISLD	$102\,^{3}/_{16}$	2
BTRD	$102\,^{1}/_{16}$	10	INCA	$102\,^{3}/_{16}$	5
RSSF	102	10	DKNY	$102\,^{3}/_{16}$	1
MONT	102	10	SHWD	$102\,^{1}/_{4}$	10
PWJC	$101\,^{15}/_{16}$	10	FBCO	$102\,^{1}/_{4}$	1
PRUS	$101\,^{15}/_{16}$	1	MWSE	$102\,^{1}/_{4}$	10
DKNY	$101\,^{15}/_{16}$	1	KCMO	$102\,^{1}/_{4}$	10
BRUT	$101\,^{7}/_{8}$	5	SLKC	$102\,^{1}/_{4}$	1

Downward Momentum

Market Maker Leaves Best Bid

BID			ASK		
GSCO	$102\,^{1}/_{16}$	10	1. Goldman @ $102\,^{1}/_{16}$ → $02\,^{3}/_{16}$		10
REDI	$102\,^{1}/_{16}$	22	ISLD	$102\,^{3}/_{16}$	2
SBSH	$102\,^{1}/_{16}$	10	INCA	$102\,^{3}/_{16}$	5
INCA	$102\,^{1}/_{16}$	16	DKNY	$102\,^{3}/_{16}$	1
BTRD	$102\,^{1}/_{16}$	10	GSCO	$102\,^{1}/_{4}$	10
RSSF	102	10	SHWD	$102\,^{1}/_{4}$	10
MONT	102	10	FBCO	$102\,^{1}/_{4}$	1
PWJC	$101\,^{15}/_{16}$	10	MWSE	$102\,^{1}/_{4}$	10
DKNY	$101\,^{15}/_{16}$	1	KCMO	$102\,^{1}/_{4}$	10
BRUT	$101\,^{7}/_{8}$	5	SLKC	$102\,^{1}/_{4}$	1

Upward Momentum

Market Maker Leaves Lowest Offer

BID			ASK		
REDI	102 $^{1}/_{16}$	22	REDI	102 $^{3}/_{16}$	10
SBSH	102 $^{1}/_{16}$	10	ISLD	102 $^{3}/_{16}$	2
INCA	102 $^{1}/_{16}$	16	INCA	102 $^{3}/_{16}$	5
BTRD	102 $^{1}/_{16}$	10	DKNY	102 $^{3}/_{16}$	1
RSSF	102	10	SHWD	102 $^{1}/_{4}$	10
MONT	102	10	FBCO	102 $^{1}/_{4}$	1
PWJC	101 $^{15}/_{16}$	10	MWSE	102 $^{1}/_{4}$	10
PRUS	101 $^{15}/_{16}$	1	KCMO	102 $^{1}/_{4}$	1
DKNY	101 $^{15}/_{16}$	1	SLKC	102 $^{1}/_{4}$	1
			GSCO	102 $^{11}/_{16}$	10

2. Market Maker Leaves Lowest Offer → GSCO

Downward Momentum

Market Maker Leaves Best Bid

BID			ASK		
REDI	102 $^{1}/_{16}$	22	REDI	102 $^{3}/_{16}$	10
SBSH	102 $^{1}/_{16}$	10	ISLD	102 $^{3}/_{16}$	2
INCA	102 $^{1}/_{16}$	16	INCA	102 $^{3}/_{16}$	5
BTRD	102 $^{1}/_{16}$	10	DKNY	102 $^{3}/_{16}$	1
RSSF	102	10	GSCO	102 $^{1}/_{4}$	10
MONT	102	10	SHWD	102 $^{1}/_{4}$	10
PWJC	101 $^{15}/_{16}$	10	FBCO	102 $^{1}/_{4}$	1
DKNY	101 $^{15}/_{16}$	1	MWSE	102 $^{1}/_{4}$	10
BRUT	101 $^{7}/_{8}$	5	KCMO	102 $^{1}/_{4}$	10
GSCO	101 $^{9}/_{16}$	10			

2. Market Maker Leaves Best Bid → GSCO

continues

Level II Momentum *(continued)*

Upward Momentum

Market Maker Stays at Best Bid After SOESed

BID				ASK		
REDI	102 1/16	22		REDI	102 3/16	10
GSCO	102 1/16	10			QUOTE	
INCA	102 1/16	16		Last	Share	
BTRD	102 1/16	10		102 1/2	10	
RSSF	102	10		102 1/2	6	
MONT	102	10		102 1/4	5	
PWJC	101 15/16	10		102 1/4	10	
PRUS	101 15/16	1		102 1/16	10	
DKNY	101 15/16	1		MWSE	102 1/4	10
BRUT	101 7/8	5		KCMO	102 1/4	10
				SLKC	102 1/4	1

Downward Momentum

Market Maker Stays at Lowest Offer After SOESed

BID				ASK		
REDI	102 1/16	22		REDI	102 3/16	10
BTRD	QUOTE			GSCO	102 3/16	10
INCA	Last	Share		ISLD	102 3/16	2
BTRD	102 5/16	4		INCA	102 3/16	5
RSSF	102 5/16	10		DKNY	102 3/16	1
MONT	102 1/4	6		SHWD	102 1/4	10
PWJC	102 1/4	10		FBCO	102 1/4	1
PRUS	102 3/16	8		MWSE	102 1/4	10
PRUS	101 15/16	1		KCMO	102 1/4	10
DKNY	101 15/16	1		SLKC	102 1/4	1
BRUT	101 7/8	5				

Upward Momentum

Market Maker Stays at Best Bid After SOESed

BID

REDI	102 1/16	22
GSCO	102 1/16	10
INCA	102 1/16	16
BTRD	102 1/16	10
R	*Orders at 102 1/16 for 1,000 shares are probable SOES orders*	
MONT	102	10
PWJC	101 15/16	10
PRUS	101 15/16	1
DKNY	101 15/16	1
BRUT	101 7/8	5

ASK

REDI	102 3/16	10
QUOTE		10

Last	Share
102 1/16	10
102 1/16	10
102 1/16	10
102 1/16	10
102 1/16	10

MWSE	102 1/4	10
KCMO	102 1/4	10
SLKC	102 1/4	1

Downward Momentum

Market Maker Stays at Lowest Offer After SOESed

BID

REDI	102 1/16	22
BTRD	QUOTE	
INCA		
BTRD		
RSSF		
MONT		
PWJC		
PRUS	101 15/16	1
DKNY	101 15/16	1
BRUT	101 7/8	5

Last	Share
102 3/16	10
102 3/16	10
102 3/16	10
102 3/16	10
102 3/16	10

ASK

REDI	102 3/16	10
GSCO	102 3/16	10
ISLD	102 3/16	2
INCA	102 3/16	5
		1
	102 1/4	10
FBCO	102 1/4	1
MWSE	102 1/4	10
KCMO	102 1/4	10
SLKC	102 1/4	1

Orders at 102 3/16 for 1000 shares are probable SOES orders

continues

Level II Momentum (continued)

Upward Momentum

Market Maker/ECN Shows Size on Best Bid

BID			ASK		
REDI	$102\,^1/_{16}$	22	REDI	$102\,^3/_{16}$	10
GSCO	$102\,^1/_{16}$	10	ISLD	$102\,^3/_{16}$	2
SBSH	$102\,^1/_{16}$	10	INCA	$102\,^3/_{16}$	5
INCA	$102\,^1/_{16}$	160	Market Maker/ECN Shows Size on Best Bid	^{16}	1
ISLD	$102\,^1/_{16}$	140		$_4$	10
RSSF	102	10	SHWD	$102\,^1/_4$	10
MONT	102	10	FBCO	$102\,^1/_4$	1
PWJC	$101\,^{15}/_{16}$	10	MWSE	$102\,^1/_4$	10
DKNY	$101\,^{15}/_{16}$	1	KCMO	$102\,^1/_4$	10
BRUT	$101\,^7/_8$	5	SLKC	$102\,^1/_4$	1

Downward Momentum

Market Maker/ECN Shows Size on Lowest Offer

BID			ASK		
REDI	$102\,^1/_{16}$	22	REDI	$102\,^3/_{16}$	10
GSCO	$102\,^1/_{16}$	10	GSCO	$102\,^3/_{16}$	10
SBSH	$102\,^1/_{16}$	10	ISLD	$102\,^3/_{16}$	120
INCA	Market Makers/ECN Shows Size On Lowest Offer		INCA	$102\,^3/_{16}$	180
ISLD			DKNY	$102\,^3/_{16}$	160
RSSF	102	10	SHWD	$102\,^1/_4$	10
MONT	102	10	FBCO	$102\,^1/_4$	1
PWJC	$101\,^{15}/_{16}$	10	MWSE	$102\,^1/_4$	10
DKNY	$101\,^{15}/_{16}$	1	KCMO	$102\,^1/_4$	10
BRUT	$101\,^7/_8$	5	SLKC	$102\,^1/_4$	1

ECN Size (particularly Instinet-INCA) Ticks Up on Best Bid

BID			ASK		
REDI	102 1/16	22	REDI	102 3/16	10
GSCO	102 1/16	10	ISLD	102 3/16	2
SBSH	102 1/16	10	INCA	102 3/16	5
INCA	102 1/16	16	GSCO	102 1/4	10
BTRD	102 1/16	10	SHWD	102 1/4	10
RSSF	102	10	FBCO	102 1/4	1
MONT	102	10	MWSE	102 1/4	10
PWJC	101 15/16	10	KCMO	102 1/4	10
DKNY	101 15/16	1	SLKC	102 1/4	1
BRUT	101 7/8	5			

1. Instinet Size @ 102 1/16 ← (INCA)

ECN Size (particularly Instinet-INCA) Ticks Down on Lowest Offer

BID			ASK		
REDI	102 1/16	22	REDI	102 3/16	10
SBSH	102 1/16	10	GSCO	102 3/16	10
INCA	102 1/16	16	ISLD	102 3/16	2
BTRD			INCA	102 3/16	180
RSSF	102	10	DKNY	102 3/16	1
MONT	102	10	SHWD	102 1/4	10
PWJC	101 15/16	10	FBCO	102 1/4	1
PRUS	101 15/16	1	MWSE	102 1/4	10
DKNY	101 15/16	1	KCMO	102 1/4	10
BRUT	101 7/8	5	SLKC	102 1/4	1

1. Instinet Size @ 102 3/16 → (INCA)

continues

Level II Momentum (continued)

Upward Momentum

ECN Size (particularly Instinet-INCA) Ticks Up on Best Bid

BID			ASK		
				2. Instinet Size Ticks Up on Best Bid	
INCA	102 1/8	140	ISLD	102 3/16	2
REDI	102 1/16	22	INCA	102 3/16	5
GSCO	102 1/16	10	DKNY	102 3/16	1
SBSH	102 1/16	10	GSCO	102 1/4	10
BTRD	102 1/16	10	SHWD	102 1/4	10
RSSF	102	10	FBCO	102 1/4	1
MONT	102	10	MWSE	102 1/4	10
PwJC	101 15/16	10	KCMO	102 1/4	10
DKNY	101 15/16	1	SLKC	102 1/4	1
BRUT	101 7/8	5			

Downward Momentum

ECN Size (particularly Instinet-INCA) Ticks Down on Lowest Offer

BID			ASK		
				2. Instinet Size Ticks Down on Lowest Offer	160
REDI	102 1/16		REDI	102 3/16	10
SBSH	102 1/16	10	GSCO	102 3/16	10
INCA	102 1/16	16	ISLD	102 3/16	2
BTRD	102 1/16	10	DKNY	102 3/16	1
RSSF	102	10	SHWD	102 1/4	10
MONT	102	10	FBCO	102 1/4	1
PWJC	101 15/16	10	MWSE	102 1/4	10
PRUS	101 15/16	1	KCMO	102 1/4	10
DKNY	101 15/16	1	SLKC	102 1/4	1
BRUT	101 7/8	5			

Prints Go Off Above Lowest Offer

BID			ASK		
REDI	102 1/16	22	REDI	102 3/16	10
GSCO	QUOTE		BTRD	102 3/16	10
INCA			ISLD	102 3/16	2
BTRD			INCA	102 3/16	5
RSSF			DKNY	102 3/16	1
MONT			SHWD	102 1/4	10
PWJC			FBCO	102 1/4	1
PRUS	101 15/16	1	MWSE	102 1/4	10
DKNY	101 15/16	1	KCMO	102 1/4	10
BRUT	101 7/8	5	SLKC	102 1/4	1

QUOTE

Last	Share
102 3/16	3
102 3/16	8
102 1/4	10
102 1/4	8
102 3/16	10

Prints Go Off Below Best Bid

BID			ASK		
REDI	102 1/16	22	REDI	102 3/16	10
GSCO	102 1/16	10	BTRD	QUOTE	10
INCA	102 1/16	16	ISLD		2
BTRD	102 1/16	10	INCA		5
RSSF	102	10	DKNY		1
MONT	102	10	SHWD		10
PWJC	101 15/16	10	FBCO		1
PRUS	101 15/16	1	MWSE	102 1/4	10
DKNY	101 15/16	1	KCMO	102 1/4	10
BRUT	101 7/8	5	SLKC	102 1/4	1

QUOTE

Last	Share
102 1/16	4
102 1/16	6
102	10
102	7
102 15/16	10

continues

Level II Momentum *(continued)*

Upward Momentum

Prints Go Off Above Lowest Offer

BID				ASK		
REDI	102 1/16	22		REDI	102 3/16	10
GSCO		0		BTRD	102 3/16	10
INCA		6		ISLD	102 3/16	2
BTRD		0		INCA	102 3/16	5
RSSF				SHWD	102 1/4	10
MONT		0		FBCO	102 1/4	1
PWJC		0		MWSE	102 1/4	10
PRUS	101 15/16	1		KCMO	102 1/4	10
DKNY	101 15/16	1		SLKC	102 1/4	1
BRUT	101 7/8	5				

Prints Go Off Above Lowest Offer

QUOTE

Last	Share
102 1/4	10
104 1/4	8
102 3/16	10
102 1/4	10
102 1/4	10

Downward Momentum

Prints Go Off Below Best Bid

BID				ASK		
REDI	102 1/16	22		REDI	102 3/16	10
GSCO	102 1/16	10		BTRD	102 3/16	10
INCA	102 1/16	16		ISLD	102 3/16	2
BTRD	102 1/16	10		INCA		5
RSSF	102			SHWD		
MONT	102	10		FBCO		1
PWJC	101 15/16	10		MWSE	102 1/4	10
PRUS	101 15/16	1		KCMO	102 1/4	10
DKNY	101 15/16	1		SLKC	102 1/4	1
BRUT	101 7/8	5				

Prints Go Off Below Best Bid

QUOTE

Last	Share
102	10
102	7
102 1/16	10
102	10
102	10

Initiate Trade by Lifting Offers of Strong Stocks/Hitting Bids of Weak Stocks via SOES and ECNs. Use Relative Strength.

Technical Momentum

Upward Momentum	*Downward Momentum*
Stock Makes Higher Highs/Higher Lows	Stock Makes Lower Lows/Lower Highs
Stock Breaks Up Past Open, Previous Day's Close, Previous Day's High, Day's High, 52-Week High	Stock Breaks Down Past Open, Previous Day's Close, Previous Day's Low, Day's Low, 52-Week Low

Initiate Trade by Lifting Offers of Strong Stocks/Hitting Bids of Weak Stocks via SOES and ECNs. Use Relative Strength.

Market Momentum

Upward Momentum	*Downward Momentum*
S+P Futures Tick Up	S+P Futures Tick Down
Nasdaq Futures Tick Up	Nasdaq Futures Tick Down
Advancers to Decliners Improving	Decliners to Advancers Improving
NYSE Up—Ticks Improving	NYSE Down—Ticks Improving
Dow Ticks Up	Dow Ticks Down
Nasdaq Composite Ticks Up	Nasdaq Composite Ticks Down
Nasdaq 100 Ticks Up	Nasdaq 100 Ticks Down
Philadelphia Semiconductor Index Ticks Up	Philadelphia Semiconductor Index Ticks Down
Market Leaders Tick Up (such as, MSFT, IBM, etc.)	Market Leaders Tick Down (such as, MSFT, IBM, etc.)

Level II Stopped Momentum/Saturation

Stopped Downward Momentum

ECN Shows Size on Best Bid

BID			ASK		
REDI	102 1/16	22	REDI	102 3/16	10
GSCO	102 1/16	10	ISLD	102 3/16	2
SBSH	102 1/16	10	INCA	102 3/16	5
INCA	102 1/16	160	Market Maker/ECN Shows Size on Best Bid		6
ISLD	102 1/16	140			10
RSSF	102	10	SHWD	102 1/4	10
MONT	102	10	FBCO	102 1/4	1
PWJC	101 15/16	10	MWSE	102 1/4	10
DKNY	101 15/16	1	KCMO	102 1/4	10
BRUT	101 7/8	5	SLKC	102 1/4	1

Stopped Upward Momentum

ECN Shows Size on Lowest Offer

BID			ASK		
REDI	102 1/16	22	REDI	102 3/16	10
GSCO	102 1/16	10	GSCO	102 3/16	10
SBSH	102 1/16	10	ISLD	102 3/16	120
INCA	102 1/16	160	Market Maker/ECN Shows Size on Lowest Offer		180
ISLD	102 1/16	140			160
RSSF	102	10	SHWD	102 1/4	10
MONT	102	10	FBCO	102 1/4	1
PWJC	101 15/16	10	MWSE	102 1/4	10
DKNY	101 15/16	1	KCMO	102 1/4	10
BRUT	101 7/8	5	SLKC	102 1/4	1

Stopped Downward Momentum					
ECN Size (particularly Instinet-INCA) Ticks Up on Best Bid					
BID			**ASK**		
REDI	102 1/16	22	REDI	102 3/16	10
GSCO	102 1/16	10	ISLD	102 3/16	2
SBSH	102 1/16	10	INCA	102 3/16	5
INCA	102 1/16	160 ◄	1. Instinet Size @ 102 1/16		1
BTRD	102 1/16	10	GSCO	102 1/4	10
RSSF	102	10	SHWD	102 1/4	10
MONT	102	10	FBCO	102 1/4	1
PWJC	101 15/16	10	MWSE	102 1/4	10
DKNY	101 15/16	1	KCMO	102 1/4	10
BRUT	101 7/8	5	SLKC	102 1/4	1

Stopped Upward Momentum					
ECN Size (particularly Instinet-INCA) Ticks Down on Lowest Offer					
BID			**ASK**		
REDI	102 1/16	22	REDI	102 3/16	10
SBSH	102 1/16	10	GSCO	102 3/16	10
INCA	102 1/16	16	ISLD	102 3/16	2
BTRD	1. Instinet Size @ 102 3/16		► INCA	102 3/16	180
RSSF	102	10	DKNY	102 3/16	1
MONT	102	10	SHWD	102 1/4	10
PWJC	101 15/16	10	FBCO	102 1/4	1
PRUS	101 15/16	1	MWSE	102 1/4	10
DKNY	101 15/16	1	KCMO	102 1/4	10
BRUT	101 7/8	5	SLKC	102 1/4	1

continues

Level II Stopped Momentum/Saturation (continued)

Stopped Downward Momentum

ECN Size (particularly Instinet-INCA) Ticks Up on Best Bid

BID

Symbol	Price	Size
INCA	102 1/8	140 →
REDI	102 1/16	22
GSCO	102 1/16	10
SBSH	102 1/16	10
BTRD	102 1/16	10
RSSF	102	10
MONT	102	10
PWJC	101 15/16	10
DKNY	101 15/16	1
BRUT	101 7/8	5

ASK

2. Instinet Size Ticks Up on Best Bid

Size	Price	Symbol
2	102 3/16	ISLD
5	102 3/16	INCA
1	102 3/16	DKNY
10	102 1/4	GSCO
10	102 1/4	SHWD
1	102 1/4	FBCO
10	102 1/4	MWSE
10	102 1/4	KCMO
1	102 1/4	SLKC

Stopped Upward Momentum

ECN Size (particularly Instinet-INCA) Ticks Down on Lowest Offer

BID

Symbol	Price	Size
REDI	102 1/16	10
SBSH	102 1/16	10
INCA	102 1/16	16
BTRD	102 1/16	10
RSSF	102	10
MONT	102	10
PWJC	101 15/16	10
PRUS	101 15/16	1
DKNY	101 15/16	1
BRUT	101 7/8	5

ASK

2. Instinet Size Ticks Down on Lowest Offer

Symbol	Price	Size
REDI	102 3/16	→ 160
GSCO	102 3/16	10
ISLD	102 3/16	10
DKNY	102 3/16	2
SHWD	102 1/4	1
FBCO	102 1/4	10
MWSE	102 1/4	1
KCMO	102 1/4	10
SLKC	102 1/4	10

Level II Stopped Momentum/Saturation

Stopped Downward Momentum

Market Maker Stays at Best Bid After SOESed

BID			ASK		
REDI	102 1/16	22	REDI	102 3/16	10
GSCO	102 1/16	10	BTRI		10
INCA	102 1/16	16	ISLD		2
BTRD	102 1/16	10	INCA		5
RSSF	102	10	DKN		1
MONT	102	10	SHW		10
PWJC	101 15/16	10	FBC		1
PRUS	101 15/16	1	MWSE	102 1/4	10
DKNY	101 15/16	1	KCMO	102 1/4	10
BRUT	101 7/8	5	SLKC	102 1/4	1

QUOTE

Last	Share
102 1/2	10
102 1/2	6
102 1/4	5
102 1/4	10
102 1/16	10

Stopped Upward Momentum

Market Maker Stays at Lowest Offer After SOESed

BID			ASK		
REDI	102 1/16	22	REDI	102 3/16	10
BTRD		10	GSCO	102 3/16	10
INCA		16	ISLD	102 3/16	2
BTRD		10	INCA	102 3/16	5
RSSF		10	DKNY	102 3/16	1
MONT		10	SHWD	102 1/4	10
PWJC		10	FBCO	102 1/4	1
PRUS	101 15/16	1	MWSE	102 1/4	10
DKNY	101 15/16	1	KCMO	102 1/4	10
BRUT	101 7/8	5	SLKC	102 1/4	1

QUOTE

Last	Share
102 5/16	4
102 5/16	10
102 1/4	6
102 1/4	10
102 3/16	8

continues

Level II Stopped Momentum/Saturation (continued)

Upward Momentum

Market Maker Stays at Best Bid After SOESed

BID			ASK		
REDI	102 1/16	22	REDI	102 3/16	10
GSCO	102 1/16	10			
INCA	102 1/16	16			
BTRD	102 1/16	10			

Orders at 102 1/16 for 1,000 shares are probable SOES orders

QUOTE		
Last		**Share**
102 1/16		10
102 1/16		10
102 1/16		10
102 1/16		10
102 1/16		10

BID			ASK		
MONT	102	10	MWSE	102 1/4	10
PWJC	101 15/16	10	KCMO	102 1/4	10
PRUS	101 15/16	1	SLKC	102 1/4	1
DKNY	101 15/16	1			
BRUT	101 7/8	5			

Downward Momentum

Market Maker Stays at Lowest Offer After SOESed

BID			ASK		
REDI	102 1/16	22	REDI	102 3/16	10
BTRD			GSCO	102 3/16	10
INCA			ISLD	102 3/16	2
BTRD			INCA	102 3/16	5
RSSF					
MONT					

Orders at 102 3/16 for 1000 shares are probable SOES orders

QUOTE		
Last		**Share**
102 3/16		10
102 3/16		10
102 3/16		10
102 3/16		10
102 3/16		10

BID			ASK		
PWJC		1		102 1/4	1
PRUS	101 15/16	1	FBCO	102 1/4	1
DKNY	101 15/16	1	MWSE	102 1/4	10
BRUT	101 7/8	5	KCMO	102 1/4	10
			SLKC	102 1/4	1

Level II Stopped Momentum/Saturation *(continued)*

Stopped Downward Momentum

Axe Reappears on Best Bid

BID		ASK		
REDI	$102\,^1/_{16}$	22	REDI	$102\,^3/_{16}$	10
KCMO	$102\,^1/_{16}$	10	ISLD	$102\,^3/_{16}$	2
SBSH	$102\,^1/_{16}$	10	INCA	$102\,^3/_{16}$	5
INCA	$102\,^1/_{16}$	16	DKNY	$102\,^3/_{16}$	1
BTRD	$102\,^1/_{16}$	10	GSCO	$102\,^1/_4$	10
RSSF	102	10	SHWD	$102\,^1/_4$	10
MONT	102	10	FBCO	$102\,^1/_4$	1
PWJC	$101\,^{15}/_{16}$	10	MWSE	$102\,^1/_4$	10
DKNY	$101\,^{15}/_{16}$	1	KCMO	$102\,^1/_4$	10
BRUT	$101\,^7/_8$	5	SLKC	$102\,^1/_4$	1

1. Goldman Not On Screen

Stopped Upward Momentum

Axe Reappears on Best Bid

BID		ASK		
REDI	$102\,^1/_{16}$	22	REDI	$102\,^3/_{16}$	10
KCMO	$102\,^1/_{16}$	10	RSSF	$102\,^3/_{16}$	10
SBSH	$102\,^7/_{16}$	10	ISLD	$102\,^3/_{16}$	2
INCA	$102\,^1/_{16}$	16	INCA	$102\,^3/_{16}$	5
BTRD	$102\,^1/_{16}$	10	DNKY	$102\,^3/_{16}$	1
RSSF	102	10	SHWD	$102\,^1/_4$	10
MONT	102	10	FBCO	$102\,^1/_4$	1
PWJC	$101\,^{15}/_{16}$	10	MWSE	$102\,^1/_4$	10
DKNY	$101\,^{15}/_{16}$	1	KCMO	$102\,^1/_4$	10
BRUT	$101\,^7/_8$	5	SLKC	$102\,^1/_4$	1

1. Goldman Not On Screen

Level II Stopped Momentum/Saturation (continued)

Stopped Downward Momentum

Axe Reappears on Lowest Offer

BID			ASK		
GSCO	102 1/16	10	2. Axe Reappears on Best Bid ▸		10
REDI	102 1/16	22	ISLD	102 3/16	2
KCMO	102 1/16	10	INCA	102 3/16	5
SBSH	102 1/16	10	DNKY	102 3/16	1
INCA	102 1/16	10	GSCO	102 1/4	10
BTRD	102 1/16	10	SHWD	102 1/4	10
RSSF	102	10	FBCO	102 1/4	1
MONT	102	10	MWSE	102 1/4	10
PWJC	101 15/16	10	KCMO	102 1/4	10
DKNY	101 15/16	1	SLKC	102 1/4	1

Stopped Upward Momentum

Axe Reappears on Lowest Offer

BID			ASK		
R[2. Axe Reappears On Lowest Offer ▸			GSCO	102 3/16	10
KCMO	102 1/16	10	REDI	102 3/16	10
SBSH	102 1/16	10	RSSF	102 3/16	10
INCA	102 1/16	10	ISLD	102 3/16	2
BTRD	102 1/16	10	INCA	102 3/16	5
RSSF	102	10	DKNY	102 3/16	1
MONT	102	10	SHWD	102 1/4	10
PWJC	101 15/16	10	FBCO	102 1/4	1
DKNY	101 15/16	1	MWSE	102 1/4	10
BRUT	101 7/8	5	KCMO	102 1/4	10

Stopped Downward Momentum	Stopped Upward Momentum
Rhythm/Pace of Downward Prints Slowing	Rhythm/Pace of Upward Prints Slowing

Initiate Long Trades by Bidding for Strong Stocks on the Bid or Between the Spread (*acting like a market maker*) via an ECN. Wait for Pullback of One-Third of the Average Trading Range of the Previous Eight Days. Use Relative Strength. Initiate Short Trades by Offering Weak Stocks on the Offer or Between the Spread via an ECN. Wait for Bounce of One-Third of the Average Trading Range of the Previous Eight Days. Use Relative Strength.

Technical Stopped
Momentum/Saturation

- Anticipate Market Maker Counter Trend at 9:50.

- Anticipate Stopped Momentum/Saturation by Knowing Where the Movement Started and the Typical Levels the Stock Trades.

- Anticipate Stopped Momentum/Saturation at Open, Previous Day's Close, Previous Day's High/Low, Day's High/Low, 52-Week High/Low.

- Anticipate Stopped Momentum/Saturation After a Change in the Uptick/Downtick of the Stock.

- Also Anticipate Stopped Momentum/Saturation Especially at Whole Numbers, Also at the $1/2$, Somewhat at the $1/4$, $3/4$.

8

LEARNING TO THINK LIKE A TRADER

THE FOUNDATION OF SUCCESSFUL TRADING is the right perspective, enjoined with the right mental attitude. They are correlative, and at the deepest levels of trading, are indistinguishable.

Part 1: The Psychology of Trading

The Tulip

The tulip was brought to Europe from the Middle East in 1559. By 1634, the Dutch were so obsessed with tulips that they could think of almost nothing else. The flowers were even bought and sold in the stock markets of numerous cities. People from around the world were paying astronomical prices for even the most common species, feeling assured that they could turn around and sell their newly acquired tulips at 100 percent profit within days. Money cascaded into Holland from all over the globe.

Eventually, prices rose so high that fear began to spread that some people who were buying tulips were going to lose big pots of money. As this realization spread, the price of tulips plummeted, and more and more people defaulted on their contracts, refusing to pay the amount they had agreed to because prices were now so much lower. Unhappy sellers turned to the courts for help, but judges said they did not deal with what they termed "gambling transactions." So, the people who couldn't find buyers were now stuck with their pretty petals, and many people went broke.

What does this true story tell you? It should tell you, if you are wise enough to listen, that two emotions rule the market: greed and fear, and that you, as a trader, cannot afford to indulge yourself in either one. Traders who are afraid, greedy, or both, will let emotions cloud their judgment. If you lose your ability to judge a situation in a steely-eyed way, you will lose money, probably a lot of money, as a trader. You also can do great emotional harm to yourself by trading out of fear.

Here is why this chapter is essential to your development as a trader: mastering the information in the preceding chapters is important, but mastering your own mind and the principles of risk management are even more crucial. If you had no strategy but strict discipline, you'd generally end up with more money than the trader who has great strategy but no discipline.

Fear and greed

The first part of yourself that you must master is your fear. There are several kinds of fear, and you can't afford to give into any of them, even though they're all legitimate. You could be afraid of losing money, not making as much money as possible, missing a good trade, or even being wrong. Tough. All those things are likely to happen to you, and if you dwell on them you'll never become a good trader.

You must not describe your trades as good or bad. Instead, think of them as either required trades—ones which your personal sys tem says you must do, no matter how they turn out—or lessons. These trades are the ones which are made from a plan that doesn't work well, and your tuition for that education was making those trades. So what you do is change your system to adapt to your new knowledge. That's how traders get better, by refining, refining, refining.

In fact, you cannot afford to let your emotions get in the way of your trading at all. You must replace your greed and fear—all your emotions, in fact—with discipline. You must trade using the system you have worked out for yourself, always eyeing whether it's working or what improvements you could make. Period. That's it. If you let your emotions consume you, or even intrude on your thinking, you will not be focusing on your system, and that's where your attention needs to be. You have to go into trading every day with your mind clear and your emotions in check. You must park your emotions somewhere outside the trading room.

In fact, you must park your emotions back where you live. When you first start as a trader, you must have enough money to make sure you have the ability to withstand losses. Most traders start in the $25,000 to $50,000 range if they expect to make a living after a period of time. If you come in with less, then you're just exploring the business, and that's okay, too, as long as you don't have so many bills to pay that you have to make your trading profits quickly.

Making a Commitment

Your commitment to your trading business should not be how much you have to work with, but how much you can afford to lose.

If you have $50,000 as working capital and you decide you can afford to lose a third of it, that's a little short of $17,000.

If that $17,000 is your commitment, and you lose that amount, fold up your trading business and go do something else. Also, if you decide that you're not emotionally or temperamentally suited to being a trader, then close up shop. There's no point in making yourself miserable. No matter what you decide to do, always remember the rule that you should put only 20 percent of your money into trading, and the other 80 percent into long-term investments.

As a beginning trader, your goal is not to make money. That's right. Repeat: *your goal is not to make money; your goal is to keep from losing money.* You're going to make plenty of mistakes; even the most seasoned professionals do. But, eventually, if you stick with trading, you will learn, you will refine, and you will develop a system which fits your temperament, which works for you, and which you can use to make money.

You just have to make sure that when that time rolls around, you've got the capital left to take advantage of it. If you get hit with large losses early in the game, you'll probably be too broke to continue trading. You have to make sure that you're still in the game by the time you have figured out your personal program and your own strengths and weaknesses. You must use your personal system to trade in a disciplined, almost mechanical way, keeping as tight a leash as possible on your emotions. Successful trading is not necessarily exciting because you are using your discipline and not emotion. Most people have a very hard time exercising discipline, but that is how you will make money.

Personal Responsibility

You also must take personal responsibility. You and you alone are responsible for your successes and failures. Many people are attracted to trading for this very reason. Your income is solely based on your bottom line, not on office politics and promotion. If you find yourself blaming the market or other outside forces, take a deep breath. In trading, piling the blame anywhere but at your own door is a waste of time. And when successes happen, you should feel good, no matter how small they may be. As a beginner, you'll find that failure will visit you plenty. So enjoy the successes you achieve, even the tiny ones. While you're trading, admit your mistakes without emotion and act on that realization.

Another important element of the right frame of mind is having independent and flexible thinking. The market environment is always changing, and there is no time to call in a consultant or huddle with other traders to strategize. In developing your own system, you must think apart from the people around you. They're developing the system that is right for them, they're thinking along the lines that are good for them. What's good and right for them probably isn't precisely what's good and right for you. You must do your own analysis, reach your own conclusions, decide on your own trades. Remember, for much of the working day, it's just you and the screen. All the screen can do is give you the information you want. You have to do the rest.

Taking Care of Yourself

Remember, trading is a job which can drain you physically and emotionally. As you get ready for a new trading day, start doing good for yourself before you ever walk out your door to go to the office. How? It's advice your mother probably gave you, but it's true: eat right and exercise. Start out your day by having breakfast. During the day, have lunch. Exercise when you're not at the office. Trading is a job where you're glued to your seat for 6 ½ hours, maybe more if you're trading before and after hours. If you eat right and exercise, you will feel better, and feeling well physically can only help you. In trading, there are many emotional elements and split-second decisions. If your blood sugar is spiking up and down and the market is too, your judgment won't be at its best.

Basically, the idea is to establish a routine. It's too easy to become so consumed by the market that you skip breakfast and lunch and don't exercise. If you're not attending to your body, your mind won't be making the clear-headed decisions you must make in order to do well as a trader.

You must also nourish relationships; you must have good relationships in your life. Remember, in the long run, it's easy to burn out as a trader because the physical and emotional demands are quite real. Trading is not your garden-variety desk job. It can be lonely and isolating. You're not interacting with people. The most important relationship you have during the day is between you and the screen. That's an emotional strain you have to be prepared for.

To nourish your relationships and your mental health, you must divorce your trading from the rest of your life. If you find yourself up and fun to be around when you do well in the market, but in a bad mood, even surly and unresponsive, if you had a bad day trading, you need to snap out of it—fast. If these signs appear in your life, you're losing perspective, you're letting your trading rule your life, and that's not good for you, your relationships, or your mental health. Bottom line, you're not going to trade as well or think as clearly if your life becomes consumed by the market. So for the sake of your profits and your sanity, go get a life if you don't already have one. If you've got one, do what it takes to keep it. Your trading will be a lot better and you'll be a lot happier in the long run.

Start of the Trading Day

When you arrive at the office and before you start your trading day, make sure you stay upbeat and keep nourishing yourself with upbeat language, telling yourself that you will and can do the things you need to do, such as honoring your stops or cutting your losses. Boost your self-esteem by saying "I am . . . ," then tell yourself exactly what you are and need to be: disciplined, organized, set to make good trades, capable of following your system and learning from your mistakes, intelligent, focused, and capable of analyzing the market well.

All this preparation may seem almost irrelevant, even frivolous and straight out of a New Age handbook. It's not. If you're not in the right frame of mind, if you're not upbeat and confident, you're going to make silly, sometimes even stupid, mistakes. You will give in to your emotions and do things you shouldn't. Trading is an intense business. If you don't stoke your own ego, your own confidence, who will?

Also, don't beat up on yourself, don't sabotage yourself by telling yourself that you're stupid. When you hear yourself questioning your state of mind, stop immediately. Pause, take a deep breath, and substitute mental language which reinforces your abilities, not destroys them.

This approach is especially important when it comes to handling losses. Remember, you're going to lose, and lose a lot. Can you handle those losses without pointing your fingers at other people, recognizing that you alone are responsible for yourself? Can you accept losses without calling yourself stupid? And if you do call yourself stupid, can you choke off that critical attitude quickly by affirming positive things about yourself? If you aren't prepared to handle losses, you shouldn't be a trader.

During the Trading Day

During the day, you also must take breaks. You don't trade as well or think as well when you're consumed by one thing, even if you're a high-volume trader. If you need to take a break, then do it, even if it's just to go for a walk or have lunch. If you miss a trade or two, so be it. You're staying fresh. If you don't stay fresh, you won't make good decisions.

End of the Trading Day

After the trading day is over, to make sure you and your plan are on track, review the situation every so often. The daily review covers what happened as the result of not sticking with your own trading rules, developing a couple of alternatives which would have helped you reach a good conclusion, and then mentally rehearsing these alternatives so you can do well by yourself when a similar occasion rolls around.

The Periodic Review

The periodic review is the time to make changes in your game plan. If you're doing a lot of trades each day, then review your business plan every month; if you trade a couple of times a week, then every quarter should do.

By the way, in any overall strategy, selling is one of the most difficult arts to master. Here are some possible reasons to get out of a trade: when the reason you got into the trade is gone, when you're running out of time, when the market becomes much more volatile, when the market gets to where you wanted, and—most importantly —if the market is going against you. Remember to make your selling strategy part of your pretrading thinking and your posttrading review.

Another quality you must have is more like a scholar's: you must have an absolute, unquenchable thirst for learning. You must be humble enough to recognize that you always will have a great deal to learn, especially as a beginner, and that preconceived notions will injure you. Let the market tell you what is happening; don't become so arrogant you think the market ought to act the way you think it should. That means constantly reading, constantly tracking your personal system and every signal you use to see how well it anticipates the market. You should even keep a journal of your trades. Studying that journal will help you see what you did well and what you did badly. You also must have decided before you start trading just how much risk you're willing to assume. You'll learn more about risk management levels a little later. Learning all this will not be a pain-free experience. You will lose money along the way, and sometimes you will lose big. What will make you a successful trader is keeping the percentage and the size of your losses as small as possible. If you can just do that, you will be a winner.

Let's review:

Before, during, and after the market, keep yourself in good shape and keep your losses to a minimum.

Before you start the day, read your personal system and tell yourself a lot of good things: that you are ready to make a good trade and that you are resourceful, successful, intelligent, and patient.

When the market opens, keep upbeat, don't beat yourself up.

When the day is over, review your trades, not so you can bleed or gloat, but so you can learn what you did right and what parts of your strategy might need improvement. Then examine ways you can improve.

Remember, too, that trading could be a path to a financially rewarding career, but it is not a springboard to instant and great wealth. Don't expect that six months from now you'll be doing your trades from your personal Caribbean hideaway. That's just not going to happen.

Part 2: Risk Management

Trading Versus Investing

A trader is not an investor. Investors usually have another job and buy and sell stocks as a secondary form of income. As such, an investor's outlook tends to be broader and longer-term. A trader, however, is a trader first and foremost. Trading is a job that requires sizable commitments of both time and focus. The life of a trader's trade tends to be much shorter than that of an investor. Investors may expect to leave money in a company for five or ten years. A swing trade tends only to last for three to five days, while a day trade can last as little as one or two minutes.

Traders and investors also have different informational needs. Investors focus on a company's fundamentals, while traders stress technical analysis and chart patterns. Longer-term trades do not require round-the-clock micromanagement. Short-term trades do. Investors can read stock quotes from the paper once a day and be considered up to date on their portfolio. Traders must know at all times where their stock is. They must also know all news surrounding the stock and its sector, how it is behaving relative to the market, and the general market conditions surrounding it. It is requisite that you have access to 24-hour top-of-the-line news and quotation services. It is relatively simple to have these things, and a huge risk not to.

Develop a Personal System

Developing a personal system will be a defining process in your growth as a trader. Obviously, since you probably haven't done much trading in the past, you don't have a system. That's okay. In this section, we're going to talk about some of the foundational aspects of a trading system. We also make suggestions as to what these should be for beginners. Don't reinvent the wheel. Ninety-nine percent of successful traders use these basic principles. Stick to them.

Hope Is Dead

People standing at the craps tables in Las Vegas make lots of noise. They cry, they shout, they cheer, but they're playing with blind luck and the law of averages. The market can feel like a craps table. Resist strongly the urge to play it like one. Emotional outbursts are detrimental to a proper trading mentality. Beseeching the gods of money, pleading with your computer screen, and yelling and screaming are all very dramatic. The market doesn't care. The only thing drama does is distort your clear, mathematical, and systemic way of thinking. A trading system must be free and clear of human emotional bias. It must be mechanical, efficient, and effective. Removing emotion allows you to operate and make changes on the system as if it were a machine. Afterward, you can take it for a test spin. If it needs more work, you keep changing it. Emotions are far too difficult to analyze. Keep them far away from your trading.

Intuition

Intuition is a powerful trading tool. It takes a very long time to develop instincts you can trust. When you've reached that point, you'll have enough of your own rules for trading, and have packed enough experience into your mind, that you'll know when to break the rules. You are a very long way from that now. Don't bet on your instincts yet. Instead, stick to the system.

Some Basic Points for Beginning Traders

Below are some general guidelines to help the beginning trader with stock selection.

1. Trade where the action is—stocks with at least a 500,000 average daily volume. You want to be in a liquid stock. This allows you

to be reasonably sure you will be able to get in and out at the levels you desire. It would take on average 150,000 shares to make a market stock like Microsoft move one point interday. For stocks which are thinly traded, especially many Internet stocks, a volume of a few thousand shares could make them go up or down one point. In stocks that are illiquid, traders have to deal with the prospect of a dramatic move against them where they cannot get out of their position. This is not a variable you want to inject into your system at this time.

2. When trading the Nasdaq, look for stocks with more than eight market makers on each side of the Level II display.

3. Consider starting with listed and Nasdaq market cap stocks. You can control your losses much easier. With NYSE stocks, you can also enter stop orders.

4. Look for stocks where the bid/ask sizes tend to be larger than 100 shares.

5. Trade stocks that cost less than $100 per share. They are a lot less volatile.

6. Trade both the long and short side of the market. You must get used to the mechanics of how a short sale is made. Get used to it now while the stakes are low.

7. Trade with a strong defense. Always be aware of risk-reward potential and where your exit points and stops are.

8. *Do not lose more than 2 percent of your money on any one trade.* If you do the math, you'll see that if you have $25,000 and you are buying in 1000-share lots, you're limited to half a point before you have to sell. If you are trading 100 shares, you have a lot more leeway. You must trade the small lots the same way you would trade the larger ones: use support and resistance, have stops, and honor them all.

You will find that many of these points are interrelated. A stock with eight or more market makers will probably have a higher average daily volume. Likewise, the bid/ask sizes will tend to be larger. A liquid stock by definition has volume. You will also notice that the most liquid stocks will tend not to be the most expensive. These companies manage their stock prices via stock splits. It is healthier for a stock to move slower and thicker, than faster and thinner. This is true, even if it is going up.

Simulation

It's a good idea to familiarize yourself with the market, and get a feel for how things move before you put any money down. There is no substitute for screen time. Several years ago, people would paper-trade. They would simulate the buying and selling of stocks with a pen and paper. This method was severely flawed. Very often, when trading real money, an order to buy or sell a stock at a specific price will not get filled. The market is always moving. When paper trading, people always fill their orders at the best price. It is not an accurate way of developing a trading system. However, it does help you familiarize yourself with the computer systems.

Nowadays, software developers have released trading simulators. These too are flawed, but to a lesser degree. A simulator will attempt to create a realistic environment. You may or may not get the stock at the price you wanted, but the true learning occurs when money is down. Simulators are excellent for getting acquainted with the mechanics of the trading software. They help you become familiar with the physical movements and routine of being a trader. Trading involves enormous amounts of repetition. A simulator will help you get comfortable with that.

The simulator phase should last only a few weeks. When you feel that you know the execution system inside and out, including the locations of all the buy and sell buttons, how to route your orders, and can retrieve information easily, you are ready to ease into using real money.

Before you start trading you will need a backup plan. When your computer screen freezes and you are in a stock position, you must be able to react quickly. Be prepared for power outages, computer lockups, and circumstances when your broker is down. Overnight traders should carry their brokers' phone numbers on their person. If you are delayed in the morning because of a traffic jam or car accident, you must be able to call your broker to get out of the position. The best of systems go down. Things happen when you least expect them. If you are working with an Internet broker, you may have difficulty getting through if systems go down. Odds are, thousands of people are doing the same thing. Direct-access brokers are much easier to reach in times of crisis.

Real Money

After you've been using the simulator and have become comfortable with the routine of trading, it's time to start using real money. Since you haven't developed anything resembling a system yet, you must trade very small dollar amounts. You've got to dip your toes into the water and start paddling around a little before you learn how to swim.

The idea here is to develop a system when the stakes are low. You are not trying to make a living at this point. You are in the educational phase, and should be generating living expenses from a source other than trading. When trading, you need to be totally clear. Worrying about rent money is not going to improve your clarity. Don't worry that you are trading a small number of shares and paying relatively high commissions. These things will only distract you. Instead, focus on your performance. Think about how you are trading. Use the analytical tools provided later in this chapter.

You must trade the small stuff as if it were the big stuff. Trade to be a good trader. Avoid thinking about your trades in monetary terms. Suppose you're trading 100 shares of stock. If the stock goes against you three points you might say to yourself, "I've only lost $300," and let it ride. This is a mistake. What will happen to a system like that when you are trading 1000 shares? Or even 10,000 shares? This principle holds true for the upside as well. You may make one point in a stock and say to yourself, "I'm only up $100, I'll stay in." But would you stay in if that were a $1000 profit? How much money you are making is not the point. What is important is that you develop a successful methodology that works no matter how many shares you are trading.

When the stakes are small, your emotions are a lot less likely to get in the way, and you can be a lot more mechanical. Now is the time to develop your discipline. Oftentimes, even good traders will reduce their share sizes when they are having trouble, so they can reduce emotional attachment and fix their mistakes. Developing a methodology that works now will enable you to make bigger trades later on. The amounts of money you lose at 100 shares, even coupled with commissions, will pale in comparison to what can be made when the stakes are larger.

Managing Share Size

Start at 100 shares. Trade no more than 100 shares on each trade for a minimum of four weeks. Don't trade larger until your account is either profitable or at least not losing money anymore. This could take several months. Just keep working hard, analyzing your trading. Wait until you're either flat or profitable before moving on. What matters is that you are taking time to develop your system when the stakes are low. You will likely feel urges to increase the stakes. Doing so demonstrates a total lack of discipline. Don't trade bigger until you have your impulses well under control. Not adhering to this principle can be very costly.

Gradually Increase up to 500 Shares. When you are ready to graduate from 100 shares, increase your size to 200 shares. The stakes are doubled now. After a week of trading here, 100 shares will seem very slow and boring. Stay at 200 until you feel you have all your impulses under control, and you are stable and profitable. Now move up to 300 shares. Stay here for several weeks. If you find that you are having more trouble at these larger sizes, move back down. The ability to cut back when things are not going well is a discipline of all the greatest traders. After you find that your system is working well at 300 shares for several weeks, you are ready for 500 shares.

500 Shares. Stop at 500 shares. That's enough for awhile. Plenty of traders make very decent livings trading 500-share lots. It is advisable to trade at this level for at least three months. If you can make money consistently at 500 shares for three months, perhaps consider moving up to 1000 shares. Do not do so otherwise.

If you ignore this advice and lose big, what will happen? The pain of losing will obscure anything you might learn from this loss. If you make 100 trades and don't make or lose much, you'll learn a lot more. Remember the goal at this level: if you learn to discipline your trading here, then you can have a stronger discipline and keep a tighter leash on your emotions when the trade size is 1000 shares.

It will take an average of about 1000 trades before you might learn to make money consistently. It's your job to make sure that you've got enough money when you reach that point to still be a trader.

Most people will be either too eager or too greedy to make it that far. If you follow the advice given in this book, you will have a chance to be one of those who are in it for the long distance. That is what we want for you.

Trader Analytical Tools

There are battles (trades) and wars (overall probability). You are going to lose many battles, but you must concentrate on winning the wars. The following tools will help you keep this in perspective.

Average Cents Per Share (ACPS) Winning Trades.   This is the total profit in dollars of winners before commissions, divided by the total shares on all winning trades.

ACPS Losing Trades.   This is the total losses in dollars of losing trades before commissions, divided by total shares on all losing trades.

ACPS Overall.   This is all trades, profits, losers, and breakevens expressed in dollars, divided by shares on all trades. This is an important number. It will serve as your benchmark for trading performance. A positive number yields a profitable precommission trader. Negative results reveal the opposite. You should look at this number 50 ways from Sunday. Look at your overall trades, then do the same for morning trades, then afternoon trades. Look at the ACPS overall number for stocks traded over 50 dollars. Look at it for stocks trading certain volume criteria. Look at it on each separate day of the week. Look at it for the entire week. Look at it for the month. How do you do in winter months compared to summer months? Good traders will know the answers to all these questions. By looking so closely at this number you will find out when you trade best. Knowing your strengths and weaknesses is an important facet of successful trading.

Win Ratio.   Win ratio is the average winning trade divided by the average losing trade. The larger the number, the better. At the very least, you need your win ratio above one. This is also a very important number.

Win Ratio: Big Wins Versus Big Losses.   This number is the average winning trade of one point or more divided by the average losing trade greater than one point. If you find that your average big winner is smaller than your average big loser, then you must either cut your losses quicker or let your profits run more or possibly both. If the difference between the average big wins and the average big losses is not large enough on the plus side, you will not succeed as a trader.

Winning Percentage.   This is derived by dividing your total number of winning trades by your total number of trades. It will tell you something about your stock selection technique. A low percentage suggests that your trade selection process needs work. But a high percentage doesn't necessarily indicate a good trading strategy. A trader who amasses many small winners and has a few large losses can have a good winning percentage with a negative bottom line. Many traders strive for 60 percent winners. If the winning percentage is low, the win ratio must be high. If you have more losers than winners, the average winner must be great enough to cover the average loser; otherwise, you will eventually go out of business.

   In order to become more profitable, you must perfect your technique in all areas and then do it on the largest scale possible while maintaining performance. If we were in any other business, we would try to get as large a profit as possible and try to sell as many units of our trade while maintaining this profit margin. Thus, you must eventually trade as many shares as you can while keeping up your winning percentage and your average cents per share.

Risk Management

There are many kinds of risk, and you need to factor all of them into your analysis of a stock and a company.

Capital Risk

The biggest risk, of course, is losing all your money. This is your *capital risk*. While this is not an exact science, you can attempt to quantify this risk. As your winning percentage falls, the win ratio must rise or you will lose all of your capital. You must protect yourself from a run of unprofitable trades by adopting a system which takes into account the worst-case scenario.

Liquidity Risk

If you find yourself in a situation where you can't get out of a stock when you want to, you are being exposed to *liquidity risk*. Before entering a position you should attempt to ascertain what your liquidity risk is. Factors such as average volume, price, market conditions, and the personality of a particular stock will help you figure out your liquidity risk.

Timing Risk

Timing risk is the probability that you will make the wrong decision at the wrong time, resulting in a losing trade, or at least losing some of your profits. This is something that will improve with time. Timing risk is greatly improved as a trader gains intuitive ability. Knowing when to run from a position a split second before everyone else can be the difference between a profit and a loss.

Margin Risk

When you buy and sell stocks with down to 50 percent of their respective market values, you are trading on margin. *Trading on margin* magnifies both gains and losses on a trade relative to the principle allocated. If a stock trades at $50 and you buy one share on margin, you need to put up only $25. Thus, if the stock goes up a point, you gain 4 percent equity on your position instead of the 2 percent you would have gained had you put 100 percent of the purchasing cost down. Losses are magnified in the same way. This is margin risk. You should consider very carefully the use of margin trading. I generally would recommend it only for experienced day traders.

The Risk of Wasting Time

Time is money. Wasting time on a losing position that is not moving can be considered a risk. Oftentimes, traders will sit and stare at a losing position for hours on end waiting for something to happen. These precious hours could have been spent focusing on the market and finding better trades. If you are in a position that is not changing, perhaps the best thing is to cut it and focus on stocks where change is occurring. Don't miss good money-making opportunities praying for life to come back into your stocks.

Other

Remember the 80 percent/20 percent rule we mentioned earlier in the book? Put 80 percent of your net capital into long-term investment vehicles. Use only 20 percent for short-term trading. If you run out of trading money, at least you won't be wiped out. We want you to do well trading, but if you don't, we want your financial life—the money you use for retirement, for buying a house, and for your children's college fund—to still be intact if you ever decide to leave trading.

More Conceptual Tools

When trading, it is important to have a healthy risk reward perspective. A successful trader cannot lose two points for every one point he or she wins. This is a formula for assured destruction.

Minimum Risk Reward.   A trader should consider a minimum risk reward ratio to be 1:2. The rewards should be twice as great as the risks. There is no exact science here, but you can think about it on these terms: if a stock typically could go up two points in whatever your time frame is, then your stop loss should be one point. Another approach is to have a stop loss set at 2 percent of your net capital. Whatever that number is, multiply it by two for the amount you need to potentially make in order to justify entering the trade. If you don't feel that you can realize this potential profit, don't make the trade.

Know When to Hold Back.   Some stocks are a lot more volatile than others. Know when to trade a lower number of shares to compensate for greater risk. If you are using the 2 percent rule, high-priced stocks may force you to lower your size so that you may apply sensible stop loss parameters.

Stacking the odds.   When trading, do everything you can to stack the odds in your favor. Combine several strategies and techniques to increase your odds. Trading is really all about finding small mathematical advantages and combining them to increase your profit probability slightly more. Remember that a strategy that was working last month may not work this month. Be prepared to change with the market. Learn to assess a situation, react if necessary, and then continually reassess until action is necessary. Be smart.

Remember that if you have a tight discipline, you will keep yourself from losing money you can't afford to lose. This way you will have time to learn to trade, and have enough funds to profit from your education later on.

Learning to Sit on Your Hands.   Boredom can kill a trader. One of the hardest things to do when trading is to do nothing. It is also one of the most important disciplines a trader can have. Depending on your system, hours or even days can go by before you see something worth doing. Out of boredom, beginners will tend to force trades when there are none. This is a terrible habit that must be stemmed.

There will also be moments before you make a trade when you feel invincible. Your senses will tell you that the odds are highly in your favor here. As time goes by, these moments will increase in frequency. Learn to spot these moments and wait for them.

Scenarios to Avoid.   There are other scenarios beginning traders should avoid. Don't trade initial public offerings; they are unpredictable. Avoid stocks with spreads wider than ⅜ of a point between the bid and the offer. Avoid bulletin board stocks and stocks priced too low. For day traders and swing traders, that's below $5 a share. For investors, unless you are particularly adept at picking distressed stocks, don't go below $20 a share. Stocks are discounted for a reason. Buy quality instead, but remember not at too high a price. Stocks which are cost more than $100 a share are far too volatile for a beginning trader to handle.

Short-Term Money Management Tips

You want to keep as much of your money as you can, and make trades that put more money in your pocket. Here are some tips to help you lose less and profit more:

Use Smaller-Share Lots, and Risk Less Money.   When things are going poorly, reduce your share size. Risk less money for a while, get back on track, then step back into the game.

Don't Trade When There Is No Flow or Momentum.   If a stock seems to be floating around in limbo without rhyme or reason, don't trade it. Stocks will often do this in the middle of the day. Even if you are already in a position that starts to do this, think strongly about getting out. If you are having trouble finding stocks with momentum, look at the major news stories of the day. Big money tends to be in these stocks and keeps them moving.

Make Sure You are Hitting the Right Keys.   Make sure that you are efficient and accurate with the keyboard. As simple as that sounds, many beginning traders fumble with the keys and make trades they didn't want, or can't get in and out when they want. Your own limitations are enough without adding that of technology.

Add to a Winning Position.   *Don't add to a losing position.* If you're a swing trader, and you have a profitable position, add to it. This is known as *scaling up.* This technique dates back to Jesse Livermore (*How to Trade in Stocks*), one of the classic investment gurus.

As you know, you shouldn't risk more than 2 percent of your net capital when buying a stock. However, if the stock moves in your favor 1 to 2 percent you could add to it, but in decreasing lots. If you bought 1000 shares initially, and the stock goes up, you might buy 800 shares the next time. If it goes up another 1 to 2 percent, buy more, but only 600 shares this time. This is called *pyramiding.* Trades where the stock does continue to move in your favor will prove extraordinarily profitable when using this method.

Do Not Average Down. This is the theory that you add more to a position as it moves against you. The idea is to lower your average cost. The rule is simple for beginning traders: *do not average down.* If you are following the rule of not risking more than 2 percent of your money on any one trade, then averaging down can bump you up against that limit pretty quickly anyway. Sure, you may see a professional do it from time to time, but knowing when to break the rules comes with many years of practice. Averaging down has also put many a trading firm out of business.

If you are an experienced swing trader, you may consider adding to your position one time on the way down. Add to your position if your stock has headed down but is still above the support level, particularly if the market or its sector took the stock down. However, if the market and/or its industry group rally, and your stock does not, sell your position.

Swing Traders Should Be Hedged 3:1. If you are a swing trader, you must be hedged 3 to 1. That is, if you have 75 percent of your money in long trades, then you should have 25 percent in short trades, and vice versa.

Have Stops. You should have stops. Do not ever go into a trade without a stop loss strategy. If it's a listed stock, put your stop loss in right away. If it's an OTC stock, then have a mental stop and stick to it. If your stock is doing well, your stop should be changing. You should now enter trailing stops to protect your profits. Use a trailing stop with the expectation that at some point your stock will hit that level and you will automatically be sold out. This is a good way to remove emotion and preserve profits.

Diversify. Diversify your portfolio. The fewer stocks you have, the riskier each stock becomes. The more stocks you have, and the more sectors you are in, the more your risk is spread around. This is crucial for swing and positional trading.

Keep the Right Frame of Mind.   One service you must perform for yourself is not to be a perfectionist. It's been said that the first and last ⅛ of a point in the market have cost people more money than anything else. If you expect yourself to have exquisite timing, to always be able to sell when a stock reaches a top, and buy just at the bottom, *and* to make money on every trade, you're doomed to failure. You will pile so much negativity on yourself you won't be able to trade with a clear head.

Instead of beating yourself up for having made mistakes, focus on what mistakes can tell you? Also study your successes. What do they tell you? Handling the successes will be a lot easier than handling the mistakes. How you handle the mistakes will determine your success as a trader. Remember it is possible to do everything right according to your plan and still lose money, or enter into a statistically bad risk-reward trade and make money. We can never totally remove the element of chance. All we can do is enter into intelligent trades with favorable probabilities.

Keep a Record of Your Trading.   Keep a written log. You need to jot down the what, when, and why of every trade you make. You need to keep track of share size, profits, and prices so you can analyze your trades with the tools we've provided. Did your emotions get in the way? Tabulate how many trades were just guesses. Which ones did you feel most strongly about? How many times were you too excited when you won, and too depressed when you lost? Did you have a plan? How well did you carry it out? Why didn't you stick to it? Were you prepared for the market? Did you come in abreast of the news and events that are pertinent to your stock? Which techniques did you use? Did you combine techniques? How often? Did you repeat your mistakes? Why? Did you manage your money well? If not, what did you do incorrectly? What will you do differently tomorrow?

Learning to Think Like a Trader Review Questions

1. What percentage of your net worth should you use as risk capital for short-term trading?
   a. 20%
   b. 50%
   c. 75%
   d. 100%

2. What percentage of your net worth should you devote to investing strategies (long-term equities, mutual funds, bonds)?
   a. 5%
   b. 10%
   c. 20%
   d. 80%

3. If your profit potential is 1 point on a trade, how much should you be willing to lose?
   a. ½ of a point
   b. 1 point
   c. 2 points
   d. 5 points

4. When should you use a stop loss?
   a. Only to protect a profit
   b. Only to limit a loss
   c. To protect a profit or limit a loss
   d. After a 1-point profit or more

5. You should never risk more than _____% of your risk capital on any one trade.

   a. 2%

   b. 10%

   c. 20%

   d. 50%

6. Your minimum risk-reward ratio on a trade should be

   a. 2:1

   b. 1:1

   c. 1:2

   d. 1:10

7. Stocks with large average daily trading volume tend to be harder to trade in and out of than stocks with small volume.

   a. True

   b. False

8. When you average down, you are

   a. buying more stock at a lower price than your initial purchase

   b. buying more stock at a higher price than your initial purchase

   c. selling more stock at a lower price than your initial purchase

   d. selling more stock at a higher price than your initial purchase

9. If you are hedged 3:1 in the market with $75,000 in long positions, how much do you have at risk in short positions?

   a. $225,000

   b. $100,000

   c. $33,000

   d. $25,000

10. Stocks priced over $100 tend to be more volatile than stocks priced under $100.

    a. True

    b. False

Learning to Think
Like a Trader
Review Answers

1. A
2. D
3. A
4. C
5. A
6. C
7. B
8. A
9. D
10. A

9

FINANCIAL
PLANNING

YOU MUST HAVE A GAME PLAN BEFORE YOU start to trade. That plan starts with your overall portfolio and asset allocation. You need to have a solidly grounded long-term financial life, even if your daily life is consumed by short-term buying and selling. Although not as dynamic as your short-term trading, don't lose sight of old school wisdom. Learn to budget, save, plan for retirement, and put to work some of what you learned about Classic Investment Theory into long-term investing.

Just because much of your daily life as a trader will be consumed by decisions about whether to hold a stock for seconds, minutes, hours, days, or even weeks, doesn't mean you should ignore the long-term. You have to stay focused on the other parts of your life: buying a house, paying for insurance, providing for a family if you have one, and retirement. For such longer-term goals, you need to be thinking about putting money away for the long-term. Remember, we advise you to put only 20 percent of your money into short-term trading. The other 80 percent should be in longer-term investments, and you need to give serious consideration to how you will go about putting that money to work (see Figure 9-1).

We aren't kidding about this. Some of you may be smirking at the idea of long-term money, figuring that you will be phoning in your short-term trading orders from your yacht six months from now. That's short-term thinking gone awry. We want short-term trading to be a good long-term experience for you, and we also want you to have a solidly grounded financial life. We want traders to know how to make sure that, no matter what happens with their short-term trading money, they still have a life they can look forward to with sufficient money to make sure that it's a life they can afford. This chapter is aimed at making sure that you put your long-term money to work in the most productive way to pay for that life you want.

Dividing the Pie

You must have a plan to make sure that your assets, everything that you own which has some worth, are divided up in the way that's best for your situation. First you have to take care of the basics before you start plunking your money down into investments and

Figure 9-1. Put only 20 percent of your money into short-term trading.

stocks and bonds. Consider the Good Money Map (Figure 9-2) for putting your financial life in order.

Notice that you have a lot of matters to attend to before you ever get around to investing. There's an emergency fund, a budget, insurance, and a home mortgage to put your money into before you even consider investing. Why? Because these issues are basic to having a stable life. You want to make sure you've dealt with those issues first. Let's take them one at a time.

Creating a Budget

In order to have money to invest, you have to put a firm grip on your spending. You have to know how much money you will take in and how much you have to pay out on necessities such as rent or a mortgage, car payments, insurance of various kinds, groceries, and so on.

Solution: Make sure you follow this diagram and put money into the essentials, then move up as you create the money to do it. That's where the budget comes in. A budget is a road map showing you how to navigate the necessities such as paying bills and saving, so that you'll know how much you can afford to invest. But a budget is about your life, so you have to budget for matters that don't happen every month, but you know will happen. Such items include car repairs, property tax, insurance payments, and medical problems.

Stocks, Bonds, Real Estate, Collectibles, and Other Investments			
Mutual Funds			
Qualified Retirement Plan			
Half-a-Year's Income in Low Risk Investments			
Systematic Savings Plan to meet short-term goals, intermediate, and long-range goals			
Budget	Emergency Fund	Insurance	Home Mortgage

Source: North Dakota State University, NDSU Extension Service. Reprinted with permission.

Figure 9-2. Good Money Map.

To make a budget, you can use three different methods. There's the old pen-and-paper standby, personal financial software, or Internet calculators. If you want to use software, the most common ones are Money and Quicken. You may want to take precautions that you are doing your calculations anonymously, and not just giving personal information that will be collected and used for someone's marketing purposes.

Debt, Emergencies, and Insurance

You probably have two areas of debt which you need to examine closely no matter how good a money manager you are (followed by emergency measures and asset protection).

1. **Consumer Debt.**   You probably have a couple of credit cards, maybe you're financing a car or boat, or you have similar kinds of loans. That kind of debt is costly. You're probably paying up to 20 percent a year on some of these loans, far more than you could reasonably expect most investments to pay. Why are these kinds of loans so expensive? Because they're the riskiest, the ones on which people are most likely to fall behind or not pay altogether. The higher the risk, the higher the interest.

   If you can get rid of a 20 percent credit card debt, for example, that's as good as getting twenty percent on your money every year. You don't have to pay that interest to the credit card company, so you now have the money for yourself. To keep that kind of interest burden is to let interest payments bleed away your financial future. The more you pay to the banks and credit card companies, the less you have to make sure your short- and long-term goals will be paid for.

   The only time such debt may make sense is if you're using it to start a business or buy a home, and you expect to make money in the long run. Then the money becomes an investment, because you expect to earn more than you're paying out in interest, although of course there's no guarantee that will happen. Remember, you can't write off consumer debt, or the interest on it, from your taxes.

Every dollar of debt you pay off is like giving yourself a return of whatever interest you're paying. If you're paying 20 percent on your credit cards, paying them off is giving yourself a 20 percent return because you don't have to pay that debt anymore. There's a big bonus: the return on paying your debts is tax-free. The IRS doesn't ask you to pay taxes on interest you're not paying anymore.

2. **Mortgages.**   The principle is somewhat the same as paying off credit card debt and car loans. Consider paying down your mortgage so you're not paying the bank so much in interest. It's true that interest rates are lower than credit card debt, and the interest usually can be deducted from your taxes. However, your regular house payment goes to pay off a lot of interest and very little principal, especially in the early and middle years.

In most cases, if you add extra money to a house payment, that additional sum pays off principal. The less principal you owe, the less the bank can charge you in interest. If you add $50 a month to your regular house payment during a period of five years, you will have reduced your principal by $3000. That's $3000 less on which your banker can charge you interest.

Don't be lured by the mortgage interest tax deduction. It may not be as big a deal for you as you think. Remember, you get an automatic $4300 deduction as a single filer and $7200 as a married couple. Depending on your situation, that deduction alone could be worth more than your mortgage write-off. And if you are among those people doing really well, you lose some or all of your interest deduction anyway. Take a look at your *adjusted gross income* (AGI) (taxable income) from all sources. If it's more than $126,600 in 1999, there's a formula for how much interest deduction you lose: 3 percent times the amount by which your taxable income is beyond $126,600. You could lose as much as 80 percent of your interest deduction. By the way, the $126,600 limit is the same for married people as single filers.

Of course, there are some good reasons for not paying off your mortgage ahead of schedule. First, if paying off your mortgage is going to eat into your emergency funds (more about that in a moment), making you feel psychologically cramped and uneasy, then you shouldn't do it. Emergency money is too important to jeopardize.

There are two more tangible reasons not to pay off your mortgage ahead of schedule. The first is when you can find a situation where you get a higher return on your money than the interest you're paying on your house. If you are willing to put your money into investments which could grow and have some volatility—real estate and stocks are two possibilities—you have a decent chance to earn a greater return than the 8 percent or so that you might be paying on your mortgage. If you could earn an average 12 percent on your investments, that's 4 percentage points better than paying 8 percent interest on your mortgage, a very worthwhile trade-off.

The second reason has to do with both investing and taxes. If you're putting money into retirement accounts—that includes an *Individual Retirement Account* (IRA), Keogh, or 401(k)—those payments are write-offs on your federal and usually your state income tax. Paying off your mortgage gets you no tax benefits. Because taxes are deferred, you could actually earn a lower rate of return on your retirement investment accounts than the interest you're paying on your house and still come out ahead, largely because those payments aren't being taxed right away, so all of the money goes to work for you, not just what's left over after taxes.

3. **An Emergency Fund.** Life's path is just full of potholes. Suppose your parent, spouse, or child gets sick? What if you get sick or injured? What if you lose your job, or your stock trading activities take a deep dive and you're short of money?

You've got to be ready for the stuff that goes wrong, and that means having money you can get your hands on in a hurry. If you don't have the money, you may not be able to make an investment you know will do well for you. Worse, you may have to sell an investment you already own and really want to keep. You could even have to sell your stocks, your house, your car. You may have to give up your stock trading and go back to working for someone else.

If you do have to sell an asset, remember that you may not even get all the money you've paid for it. You have to factor in transaction costs and more. Selling stocks costs brokerage fees—and can hit you with a big tax bill, too, if you've made a lot of money on them. Selling any kind of real estate means paying a lot of transaction costs and taxes. You could wind up paying 10, 15, 20 percent or more of the price you get for stocks or real estate, in taxes and transaction costs alone. You don't want to have to shoulder those burdens at a time when you're scratching hard just to pay the mortgage.

Solution: To be able to ride out those kinds of disasters, have at least an eight-month supply of ready cash on hand. It takes time to get past disasters, and they aren't necessarily over in a month. You've got to be ready.

Incidentally, the low returns on money market funds, which is the most likely place to park your emergency money, may tempt you to put your emergency money into stocks, figuring you can get a good return, good growth, and can cash them in anytime. *Don't do it.*

The emergency fund theory works well as long as stocks are going up. What if stocks head downward? Stocks have been known to skid as much as 50 percent in a fairly short period of time. What happens to you if your emergency—whether it's being in car accident, getting a serious illness which will knock you out of work for a few months, or having a flood in your house—happens at the same time that the stock market's heading south? The worth of your emergency money fund will shrivel just at the time you need it most. Even worse, if you've done well in the market you could end up paying lots of taxes on the stocks you sell for emergency cash.

4. **Asset Protection.** Essentially, this is a way of making sure that somebody else will pay the bills or there will be cash available so you or your family don't have to spend what you've got.

   Solution: Asset protection largely involves insurance. There are two kinds you should have for when you're alive, and two for when you're dead.

   When you're alive, make sure that your policies don't have limits which are too low. Have your deductibles set where they kick in at the point where, if you had to pay the bill, it would be financially disastrous.

   One policy you'll need to help you live longer is major medical, not the little policies which cover a couple of hundred dollars a day or pay small amounts for a catastrophic disease such as cancer. You need a policy which covers all kinds of expenses and illnesses. Second is long-term disability insurance. If you or someone in your family gets sick, is in an accident, or has some kind of major disability which lasts for months or even years, where will the money come from to pay the medical and other expenses? Even if you don't have dependents, you're going to need the money if some long-lasting problem prevents you from working. Find one of these policies through your employer or professional association.

Now for the part when you're dead. People hate to face this part, but they have to. If you have anyone who depends on your income, you need life insurance; buy term life and decide how much of your income to replace. You also ought to do some estate planning, which is a way of making sure that your heirs get what you want them to have with minimal fuss from the courts and the Internal Revenue Service.

At least have a simple will. If you have a lot of assets, maybe a living trust is for you. Then again, maybe not. Check with a trusts and estates lawyer who can explain the pros and cons. You may need to do even more complex estate planning than you thought. Better to do it now than have your heirs suffer the consequences later. In order to pay for all the expenses, you'll have in the bottom line of the diagram in Figure 9-2 (emergency fund, insurance, mortgage), as well as putting money aside for other layers in your Good Money Map, you need a plan. That's what financial planning is about: figuring out how much money you have coming in, how much you will be paying out, and how much you're going to put aside for various purposes.

To do some financial planning, you need to answer several questions:

Where are you now? You can't find out where you want to go until you know where you are. You need to know what your assets are and what they are worth. Figure out how much you have in liquid assets, which are assets you own that can be cashed in pretty easily; property assets, which you can check by looking at your most recent property appraisals; the worth of your art, jewelry, and other collectibles; and how much your vehicles are worth after depreciation.

How much are you spending and for what? You need to know the ways in which you are spending so you can figure out whether you are doing right by yourself or you need to redirect where your money goes. You can use Quicken, Microsoft Money, or Prosper. Paper and pencil work well, too.

What are your goals? You must know where you want your money to get you. That means planning for the short-term (2 years or less), medium-term (3 to 5 years), and long-term (6 years and longer) checkpoints in your life. Maybe you want to take a dream vacation in two years, buy a house in five years, send a child to college in twenty years, have a well-funded retirement in thirty years. It's possible to have more than one goal toward which you're aiming.

Lay out what those goals are, so you know exactly why you're putting money away and how much you need to be setting aside. Besides, it's OK if you don't know exactly what you're putting money aside for right now. Maybe what you want ten years from now is hazy to you at the moment. That's fine. But just because you don't know what you want is no reason to skip saving and investing. You want to have the money there when you need it, even if you don't know what it's for right now.

How much money will you have to put aside and how will you deploy it in order to reach your financial goals? You can use the Good Money Map to help you diversify your financial base so your money will grow and be protected at the same time.

Once you've gone through this process, you need to decide (1) how you're going to create the money to put aside, (2) what system you will use to put it aside, and (3) how much you will save and how much you will invest.

How to create the money comes down to some basics. You can either make more money or spend less of it. If you don't see a big raise or a huge inheritance in the offing anytime soon, then it's probably easier for you to spend less. That's why you're creating a budget.

To find out where your money goes, make sure you're taking care of the necessities and seeing if you can't cut out some of the frills. By the way, you'll need to feed some information to whatever calculation method you're using, so make sure you have your check register or spreadsheet available, along with credit card statements and whatever else will show you how you're spending money. Do you need to take so many vacations? Must you eat out so much? Can you find cheaper entertainment?

You also need to know how much money you'll need to reach those goals. You need to be thinking about retirement, too. Don't forget to contact the Social Security Administration to find out how much you'll be getting from the government when you retire.

You need to understand the difference between saving and investing. Saving is essentially putting money aside to meet your short-, medium-, and long-term goals. Notice that the second tier of the Good Money Map is a systematic savings plan to meet all three goals. You've got to put the money aside before you start putting it to work. One sure way to know that you aren't really ready for this step is if you still charge a lot of things by credit card and don't pay off your bills at the end of the month. Investing is putting money to work by taking some risk but having a strong possibility of a good reward.

For your short-term goals, don't put the money at risk. Instead, put the cash into money market mutual funds, where you're likely to get higher interest than at your bank, or into *Certificates of Deposit* (CDs), where your interest is guaranteed by the bank. CDs are sold to last a specific length of time, anywhere from six months to 10 years, and offering a specific rate of interest.

Then there are money market mutual funds, which have a value of $1 per share and don't go up or down. The fund puts money into high-quality investments in order to pay interest.

What you're putting to work here is compound interest—the longer you leave the money in, the more money you get in interest. If you're getting 5 percent interest and put $100 in a CD or a money market fund, you'll have $105 at the end of the year. If you leave it in for another year, you'll get 5 percent on the $105, giving you $110.25. And so on. If you want to have $20,000 at the end of 5 years, you'll have to save $300 a month at 5 percent interest or $280 at 7 percent.

For investing, use the number 72 as a constant to determine when your money will double. If you divide the rate of return into 72; the result will tell you how many years it will take for the investment to double. A 10 percent rate of return will double in 7.2 years. A 15 percent rate of return will double in 4.8 years. And, of course, the longer you leave the money in investments, the more time it will have to double and double and double again.

You should draw several lessons here. Obviously you're better off having a higher interest rate or rate of return—you'll get more about investments in a moment—and the earlier you start the better. Whether you're saving or investing, you need to start now. Why? Just look at the numbers. If you invested $125 a month starting at age 25 and had an average 12 percent return, you'd have more than $1 million when you were ready to retire after age 65. If you started when you were 40 years old, to get the same result you'd have to sock away five times that much a month. So start now!

The third level of your Good Money Map tells you to put six months' worth of income in low-risk investments. CDs and money market funds certainly qualify. So use the CD and the money market funds for your six months' worth of income—that's your emergency fund—as well as for your short-term-goal money. The CDs and money market funds are safe. Money market funds are not insured by the government, but many of their investments are. To be supersafe, put your money into money market funds which invest only in government bonds.

Now it's time to start thinking about the top three levels of your Good Money Map as well: qualified retirement plans, mutual funds, and the top layer, which includes individual stocks and bonds, as well as real estate, collectibles, and other investments.

Asset Allocation

Asset allocation **is a fancy term for making three decisions:**

1. What percentage of your investment money will you put into stocks or stock mutual funds, what percentage into bonds, and what percentage into cash?
2. What percentage of your investment money that you put into stocks or stock mutual funds will go into U.S. companies and what percentage into foreign companies?
3. What percentage of your investment money will go into bonds, money market funds, or other cash-type investments?

Before making those three decisions, you should look at seven factors:

A. How old are you?
B. How many years do you have until you retire?
C. How much risk do you want to take?
D. How much money do you want in short-term (2 years or less), medium-term (3 to 5 years), and long-term (6 or more years) investments?
E. What are your financial goals?
F. What are the tax consequences?
G. What rate of return do you want?

We urge you to answer these questions for yourself. Your answers will do a lot to guide your own decisions.

What makes these factors so important is that they have a very real impact on how much risk you should consider handling and what percentage of your assets should be in various categories. If you take on a lot of investments which are highly volatile and risky, they have a much better chance of working out if you can ride out the wild swings up and down. The longer you can wait before you need the money, the more risk you can afford to take. When it comes to risk, though, remember the rule that only 20 percent of your money should go into short-term trading. The other 80 percent should be in long-term investments.

If you're in your 20s, you can wait a very long time before you start drawing retirement money, for example. That means you can handle a lot of risk, and you should feel comfortable putting a lot more money into growth investments such as stocks and stock funds. If you're in your 50s, you shouldn't have all your money in stocks because you're going to have to start tapping that money in ten or twenty years. You need some of your money to have low risk attached to it, and so you should have a larger percentage of your money in bonds or other cash-type investments.

Before you start carving up your assets into stocks and bonds, there's another factor you have to plug into the equation: it's called your Gut Check. No formula, no financial whiz, no table of possibilities can substitute for your own internal gauge, that voice which tells you just how much risk you yourself are comfortable taking. To describe a very complicated situation very simply, consider whether you are a go-getter investor, a conservative investor, or in-between (see Table 9-1). If you are aggressive, you would be comfortable putting a lot more of your money into stocks. If you are conservative, then you should be putting a significant percentage of your money into bonds. And if you're in-between, well, the mix of stocks and bonds would be somewhere between the two.

As to how short-, medium-, or long-term you want your investments to be, that depends on a lot of factors. They have to do with your financial goals. If you want to have $20,000 to put a down payment on a house in four years, then that is money you will peg to your medium-range investments. If you're aiming for a comfortable retirement and you're in your 30s, that's long-term money. You have to make these decisions and goals. Nobody else can do it for you.

Finally, there's the tax issue. Mutual funds or stocks which pay out big dividends mean that investment will force you to pay taxes on those payouts. However, without those payouts, you depend exclusively on the stock price to go up to make your money. For some people, that's too big a risk.

Table 9-1. Asset Allocation.

	Conservative	*In-Between*	*Go-Getter*
Short-term	All in either CDs or money markets	66% in CDs or money markets, 25% in bonds, 8% in stocks	50% in CDs or money markets, rest split between stocks and bonds
Medium-term	50% in CDs or money markets, 50% split between stocks and bonds	50% stocks, 40% bonds, 10% in CDs or money markets	60% stocks, 40% bonds
Long-term	55% stocks, 45% bonds	70% stocks, 30% bonds	100% stocks

It's a trade-off, as are a lot of aspects of stock investing, whether it's mutual funds or individual stocks. Just remember, stock prices go down as well as up, and you have to be ready to ride out the bad times.

For your long-term money, you might be a lot better off starting out with mutual funds, rather than individual stocks. Why? It reduces risk. You'll be taking plenty of risks as a short-term trader. We want you to feel comfortable that your longer-term investments are pretty safe. A mutual fund has one big advantage over you as an individual investor (and for longer-term money, remember you're an investor, not a trader): you probably won't invest in more than a dozen stocks or so. If a couple of them head south in a major way, your other stocks aren't likely to give you the kind of return which will make up the difference. Mutual funds, though, invest in a minimum of dozens, and most likely, hundreds of stocks. If they have some stocks which perform badly, they have a better likelihood of having enough other stocks doing well to still make your portfolio profitable.

Mutual funds give you three bangs for your buck. First, companies pay dividends on their stocks, and many funds pay dividends to you. Second, funds pay capital gains. Third, the net asset value of each share can go up (or down, of course).

Dollar Cost Averaging

No matter how much you're investing, one of the best ways to go about putting aside money is to use *dollar cost averaging* (DCA). This technique is simply investing a specific amount of money at a specific interval. For example, $25 a week, $100 a month, $1000 a quarter, $150 a paycheck. Use it for putting money into investments which go up and down.

There is a drawback. If your mutual funds or stocks go up and you have a lot of money parked on the sidelines, that money won't get in on the action. This technique is for people with a large amount of cash who want to transfer it safely to investments with higher risk and greater prospects of return, or who want to create an investing discipline. Make sure you put your DCA money on automatic pilot: have it arranged to take out the amount you want at the time you want and put into the place you want without your having to do anything. That way, you'll feel less guilt or pain.

Long-Term Goals: College and Retirement

If you have a child whom you'd like to go to college, you need to do some serious thinking. It's going to cost some serious money. Be prepared for sticker shock.

College

Your little tyke could cost you nearly $200,000 to send to a private college in 15 years. And that's just tuition. There's also housing, books, and incidentals.

Fortunately, there are some options available for college that aren't available for any other kind of long-term goal.

- **Pay all the tuition ahead of time.** More than 40 states let you to prepay tuition. The state takes the money and invests it, eventually paying for the costs of your child's college expenses if the child goes to college in that state. Many will let you put the money toward tuition anywhere in the country. The biggest drawbacks to these plans is that they only offer a rate comparable to a Treasury bill. You can do better on your own, usually a lot better. Use this approach only if you're not much of an investor.

- **Roth IRA.** You can take earnings out of a Roth penalty-free for higher education expenses. You won't pay a penalty but you will pay taxes on the earnings. It's not such a good idea to bite into retirement money unless you've got plenty of other retirement money to spare.

  Education IRA. It's not really an IRA because it's not aimed at retirement, but you are allowed to open this kind of account for each child or grandchild. You can put in $500 a year, but each child gets only one such account, no matter who funds it. You can only set up one of these accounts if your *modified adjusted gross income* (MAGI)—your adjusted gross income before IRA deduction or Series EE savings bond interest—is deducted. If your MAGI is lower than $95,000 if you're single, or $150,000 if you file jointly, you can create an Education IRA. Trouble is, it won't do much for you. If you're lucky, it will create about $20,000. That's not much for a tuition bill which could hit $200,000.

**HOPE (Helping Outstanding Pupils Educationally) scholarship
credit.**   You get a tax credit of up to $1500 for paying tuition
for yourself or your children in the first two years of college.
You're eligible if you have a MAGI of less than $40,000 or are
married with MAGI less than $80,000. Reduced credits are
available, too.

U.S. savings bonds.   Buy them the way you'd buy any other
bonds. If you're going to use the money for education expenses
the same year you cash in the bond, you don't have to pay
taxes on the earnings. Still, they pay less than 5 percent, and
that's not much mileage on your money toward a hefty tuition
bill.

- **Mutual fund account.**   This one is probably your best bet, and
most brokerage or mutual fund companies have college savings
plans. You'll probably grow your money much faster using this
approach. However, don't skip funding your own retirement,
either. Put money into your retirement account first. That's tax-
deferred. Investments and the returns on investments in a non-
retirement account for your children's college expenses are taxed,
so you end up paying more taxes if you pay for your kids' college and don't do much for your own retirement. When you set
up an education mutual fund account, have a high percentage in
stocks and a small percentage in bonds. As the child grows older
and gets closer to college, increasingly lower the percentage in
stocks while raising the percentage in bonds.

Retirement

Notice on your Good Money Map that qualified retirement plans
are near the top of the list. After you've made sure you're paying
your necessary expenses, after you've set up a savings plan, after
you've got money in the bank for an emergency, it's time to think
about retirement.

Whether you're an employee or own your own business, there's
a retirement plan for you. And you had better take this issue seri-
ously. People are living longer and retiring earlier, so your money
could have to last thirty or forty years after you retire. Will you have

the means to live a comfortable life after work, or will you have to be bagging groceries at your local supermarket to make ends meet?

What are retirement plans? Retirement plans are a specific kind of account which you can set up at almost any financial institution such as a brokerage or bank. When you put the money in, often that amount is deductible on your income taxes. In addition, the money is tax-deferred until you start taking it out. One thousand dollars put into a plan could save you more than $300 in taxes, if a tax break is allowed. If you don't take advantage of these tax-deductible and tax-deferred vehicles, you could be losing tens, maybe hundreds of thousands of dollars.

Don't take money out too early, though. Usually you can't take money out before you're age 59 ½. Most plans hit you with a penalty if you withdraw money before retirement. Also, start your retirement accounts young. The younger you start, the more your investments have time to grow, and the more likely it is that you will have a comfortable retirement.

After you put money into your retirement plan, you can save money and invest it in many different ways: stocks, bonds, and mutual funds. You have several different kinds of retirement plans to choose from, and you don't have to choose just one. In fact, you may have several, depending on your situation. There are four different situations which present retirement account opportunities:

1. Individual Retirement Accounts
2. Company- or organization-offered retirement accounts
3. Small business and self-employed retirement accounts
4. Annuities

Individual Retirement Accounts (IRAs). Maybe the company you work for doesn't have a retirement plan, or maybe you've put all the money allowable into the company plan and you still want to contribute more toward your retirement. These plans are for you. You can put money in an IRA until April 15 to make contributions to your IRA for the previous tax year. **Your contributions may or may not be deductible.**

1. **Standard IRA.**   If you're single and your adjusted gross income (AGI) is $32,000 or less, or if you're married and your combined income is $52,000, then you get the full deduction of $2000 a year, if you put that much into your *standard IRA*. If your income goes beyond those amounts, then the deductibility of your standard IRA deductions is phased out. However, if you aren't covered by a company pension plan, and your spouse (if you're married) isn't either, then your IRA contributions are deductible no matter how much your income. If you're going to contribute to a nondeductible IRA, make sure you have made all contributions possible to retirement accounts which are deductible first.

2. **Roth IRA.**   If you can't contribute to a deductible IRA, then a Roth may be for you. If you're single and have an AGI of less than $95,000, or married with an AGI of less than $150,000, then you qualify for a Roth. The differences between the standard IRA and the Roth are two: the Roth is always nondeductible while the standard one sometimes is, and you can take money out of the Roth penalty-free and income-tax-free for specific purposes, while that's not possible with the standard IRA. In both, the earnings that stay inside the account aren't taxed.

Figuring out whether you're better off with a standard or Roth IRA can be tricky. Consult an accountant.

Company- or Organization-Offered Accounts.   A for-profit company can offer a 401(k) account which lets you deposit up to 15 percent of your salary or $10,000 a year. The nonprofit organization can offer a 403(b), which lets you deposit up to $10,000 a year or 20 percent of your salary, whichever is smaller. In many of both kinds of plans, the employer will match your contributions up to a certain point. Generally, the employer will put in 50 cents for every dollar you put in. However, the sum of the contributions by you and your employer can't go over 25 percent of your salary, after subtracting your 401(k) contribution.

Still, you immediately make 50 cents on a lot of dollars you put into your 401(k) or 403(b). You'll probably never find another investment with such a terrific and immediate payoff.

Incidentally, if you leave a job with a 401(k), don't cash it in. If you do, you have to pay taxes and your retirement planning gets shot in the foot. Instead, transfer the account to a rollover IRA or your new job's 401(k) or 403(b). You can borrow from these accounts, but do it only in an extreme emergency. That's retirement money, and you shouldn't be messing with it unless a calamity has struck.

Small Business and Self-Employed Accounts. If you are self-employed, or if you own a small business or work for one, you have another set of choices. Just remember that if you're a small business employee, you can't set up any of these kinds of accounts. Only your employer can. However, employers who have such an account must cover their employees as well.

1. **Simplified Employee Pension Individual Retirement Account (SEP-IRA).** You can stuff up to 13.04 percent of your self-employment income up to $24,000 a year. You don't have to contribute the maximum every year. In fact, you can contribute any amount you want up to the maximum, each year.

2. **Keoghs.** Employees have to stay a minimum number of years before they qualify to get the money in their account. If the employee leaves before then, that person's account balance goes to the remaining participants. Some kinds of Keoghs let you put in 20 percent of your self-employment income up to $30,000 a year.

Annuities.   Essentially, *annuities* are insurance company guaranteed contracts that let your money grow tax-deferred. However, because the contributions are not tax-deductible, annuities are generally used only after you have put all the money you can into other retirement vehicles. They also have a nice bit of insurance: if you die before you start making withdrawals, your beneficiary is guaranteed to get at least the amount of money you first invested.

That's not much of a guarantee, but it's something. Interestingly, there's no limit on how much money you can put into an annuity. You can put in millions each year—but of course, if you could do that, you probably wouldn't need much of a retirement plan.

Just remember not to get wildly optimistic about how well your portfolio will grow. Sure, it would be nice to think your portfolio will mushroom by 15, 20, or 30 percent. However, this is not likely. In addition, as you get closer to retirement you'll want to pull back on the aggressiveness of your stock investments and start putting money into bonds and other investments which produce a fixed income. Given that likelihood, use a low average growth rate for your projections. That way, you'll be facing the reality of your situation.

Mutual Funds

The theory behind mutual funds is pretty simple: You put your money into a pot with a lot of other people, then professional managers do all the head-scratching work that you don't want to do. They do the research and the analysis; they call the companies and talk to people and buy and sell. That takes a lot of weight off your shoulders. Just because you do a lot of technical and fundamental analysis with stocks into your short-term account doesn't mean you want to put that same effort into your long-term investments. Remember, buying for the long-term is a very different kind of analysis than the short-term work you are doing.

There's another reason to put your long-term money into mutual funds: you get instant diversification. You don't have to spend a lot of time building up a portfolio of stocks or bonds. In fact, there's very little likelihood that you could diversify as much as a mutual fund. Why? Well, you don't have hundreds of millions, if not billions, of dollars to work with, and they do. Also, you don't have to go through a broker.

The return on your investment over the long haul will be a lot better than just parking your money in savings accounts, CDs, or money market funds. Just remember that the FDIC doesn't insure mutual funds.

What Is a Load?

You probably also don't want to pay a sales charge, or *load*. If you put $1000 into a fund with a 6 percent load, that means you pay the fund $60 and only $940 gets invested. Why not pick a comparable fund which lets you put all $1000 to work?

You should know there are several kinds of loads that a fund can heap on you. Avoid 12b-1 fees, which is a way for the fund to charge you for its advertising and marketing costs. Usually the fund will charge you a *front-end load*, taking its commission when it receives your money.

There may instead be a *back-end load*, which gets taken out of your money when you sell. Usually this load is reduced the longer you keep your money in the fund, disappearing altogether after five years.

There are plenty of *no-load* mutual funds you can buy directly with no broker or broker's commission. You can buy mutual funds directly from the fund family by mail. You also can do it through the Internet by using a fund family's Web site, such as Vanguard (vanguard.com) or T. Rowe Price (troweprice.com). They also let you buy numerous fund families aside from theirs through them, and even through their Web site. Some discount brokers such as Waterhouse Securities (webbroker.com) and Charles Schwab & Co. (schwab.com) will let you do the same. Not all fund families and brokers will let you buy the same mutual funds, so make sure that you can get the ones you want from the family or broker you choose if you want to buy through the Internet.

Research Your Mutual Fund

Before you put money into a fund, though, you do have to do your homework. Call the fund company's 800 number and ask for a prospectus. If you want more detail, ask for the fund's "Additional Information" as well as the prospectus. You can ask for the prospectus on the fund family's Web site, too.

There are several things you should be looking for when you read the prospectus; expenses are a big item. Any fund has expenses, but it's your job to make sure you avoid one whose expenses are too high. Generally speaking, you'll want to make sure that most of your funds have annual expenses of 1 percent or lower. Also look at fees. The Federal Securities and Exchange Commission requires a fund to list them all. Of course you want to know how well the fund has performed during the last ten years, if the fund has been around that long, or for however long the fund has been in existence. Track how well the *net asset value* (NAV) per share has fared from year to year, as well as its distributions.

You also can find out a lot of information about mutual funds online and off-line. Morningstar is a well-known and influential mutual fund ratings service. Most libraries have it, and it's well worth reading. You also can get some of the same information at morningstar.net. *Mutual Funds* magazine is a monthly publication which looks at the whole area of mutual funds in-depth. *Smart Money* is a good consumer publication which covers mutual funds, among other financial topics. It also has a data-rich Web site at smartmoney.com.

The *Wall Street Journal* has numerous investing stories and a Web site, wsj.com. Also, numerous publications such as *Business Week, Money,* and the *Wall Street Journal* have periodic in-depth comparisons and statistics of hundreds of mutual funds.

Types of Mutual Funds

You need to understand what kind of fund you're looking at and how much risk is involved (Figure 9-3). There are several different kinds of funds, starting with the safest and most conservative and progressing to the most volatile and risky. Money market funds are the safest. Bond funds have less risk than stock funds, but they still have risk. Bonds generally are for income. Another conservative kind of fund is the Balanced Fund, which has stock holdings but also has bonds and treasury bills for safety and income. Growth and income funds want a steady stream of income with some potential for growth, so they usually have companies which are growing and/or are paying good dividends. They might even have some bonds.

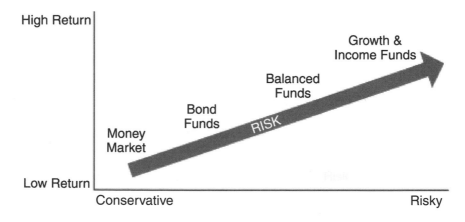

Figure 9-3. Mutual funds and risk.

Growth funds invest in bigger companies with a solid and extensive record of good earnings and growth. Aggressive growth funds focus on smaller companies, focus almost exclusively on capital growth and have little interest in income. Sector funds invest in specific aspects of the economy, such as insurance, technology, health, or telecommunications. International funds invest in companies outside the United States. They have stocks and bonds and include risks that U.S. companies don't have, including currency fluctuations and political instability. Remember, funds will focus on small, medium, or large companies, or a mixture. The small companies are the riskiest. Generally speaking, the larger the company, the less risk involved.

Getting into a Mutual Fund

When you start an account in a mutual fund, make sure you include the kind of ownership you want (individual, trust, joint, tenants-in-common), whether you want to write checks on the account, whether you want the dividends reinvested (usually a good idea), and whether you want withdrawals made automatically from a bank or some other kind of account to be deposited into the mutual fund.

Once you put your money into a mutual fund, you may want to track its NAV. Your local newspaper should have the information. It's also available in financial newspapers such as the *Wall Street Journal*.

Selling your mutual fund shares shouldn't be too hard. The funds are supposed to make this easy for you as well. You can notify the fund in writing that you want to sell, or you can call the fund company or your broker and specify how much of your holding you want sold. Federal law dictates that the fund must redeem your shares within seven days after it gets your sell order.

Bonds

Bonds often are thought of as one of the safest investments of all. That is true for some kinds of bonds, but not all. What is a bond? It's an IOU, a promise that whoever is issuing the bonds will pay your money back along with a certain amount of interest for the life of the bond, or until the issuer calls the bond back. Bonds can be issued by governments: the U.S. Treasury issues Treasury bills (auctioned periodically in denominations between $10,000 and $1 million with a maturity, or life, of a year or less; bonds, with maturities of 10 years or longer in denominations of $1000; and notes, with maturities of between 1 and 10 years and sold in denominations of $1000). Bonds can be bought directly from the federal government.

Other government entities, including states, cities, counties, and airports, as well as corporations, also issue bonds. Usually these are bought through a broker.

Bonds make money in two ways. First, they pay interest. Second, the value of the bond goes up if interest rates go down. Why? If you're holding a bond which pays 8 percent, and interest rates are at 5 percent, somebody would pay you a premium to have an income which is 3 percent higher than for bonds being issued currently. However, if interest rates go up, the value of your bond goes down. If your bond pays 5 percent and interest rates are at 8 percent, your bond isn't worth as much as the bonds paying a higher rate.

There are a couple of terms to keep in mind. *Par value* is the face value of the bond, how much the original owner paid to buy it and how much whoever issued the bond will pay to the owner when the bond expires.

Corporate bonds usually have a $1000 par value, while bonds issued by cities, states, and other government entities usually have a $5000 or $10,000 par value. The coupon interest rate specifies that the annual interest rate on the par value will be until the bond reaches maturity, which is the end of the length of time the bond is good for, whether it's a year, 10 years, 20 years, or whatever. The current yield includes factoring in the annual interest with how much the bond is selling for now. If the bond has a 9 percent coupon rate, a par value of $10,000 and a market value of $6500, the current yield (.09 × $10,000 ÷ $6500) is almost 14 percent.

Remember, bonds are less risky than stocks, but they pay less, too. To learn more about bonds, try Fidelity Brokerage (fidelity.com), which has an education section on bonds.

Financial Planning
Review Questions

Choose a corresponding letter. A letter can be used only once.

Which security would be suitable for an investor who . . .

1. is saving for retirement in 30 years?
2. is in a high tax bracket who wants to supply income?
3. has a $30,000 CD maturing and wants to put a down payment on a house in 9 months?
4. is a novice investor and wants low risk?

    a.   municipal bonds

    b.   blue-chip stocks

    c.   government bonds

    d.   money market instruments

Financial Planning
Review Answers

1. B
2. A
3. D
4. C

A

COMPLIANCE

Stock Loan/Short Sales

THE STOCK LOAN DEPARTMENT of your broker/dealer must always be called to borrow the stock before you enter a short sale. A hard-to-borrow list will be made available to you, and many broker's systems also provide a warning on your computer screen if the stock is hard to borrow. Do not override the warning or the hard-to-borrow list without prior approval of the stock loan department. Short sales made on stocks that a broker is unable to borrow may result in a buy-in. That is when the broker on the other side of the trade buys stock at their own discretion that you are responsible for.

Of course, all short sales must also be made in accordance with Nasdaq and NYSE uptick rules.

Margin Requirements

Margin rules state that all transactions must be kept at two times current equity, not four times as some people have been led to believe.

> Example: Equity $200,000 cash, no positions
>
> Buying power: $400,000

If you have overnight long or short positions there is a slightly different formula: take 30% of short position, 25% of long position, subtract both figures from equity, and double that figure to get day trading buying power.

> Example: Equity = $200,000
>
> Long $50,000 × 25% = $12,500 short, $50,000 × 30% = $15,000
>
> Subtract both figures from $200,000 = $172,500 × 2
>
> Current day trade buying power = $345,000

Overnight buying power is limited to two times your ending equity. Any total above two times equity will result in a *margin call*. There are two types of margin calls.

- *Chargeable:* Total of long positions multiplied by .25 and short positions multiplied by .30 exceeds your equity. Then your call is chargeable and must be either met in cash before they are liquidated or may be liquidated two times per six-month period. If three chargeable calls are not met with a deposit equal to or more than the call, then the account is restricted and there may not be any further calls until the restriction is lifted.

- Nonchargeable: Must meet call by settlement date by deposit or by keeping positions under two times equity by settlement date.

Example #1: $100,000 equity

$200,000 long position total

$200,000 short position total

The total requirement would be $200,000 in equity. The call would be $110,000.

$200,000 × 25% = $50,000 + 200,000 × 30% = $60,000

Total $110,000 exceeds minimum maintenance requirement and therefore the call is chargeable.

Example #2: $100,000 equity

$200,000 long position total

$100,000 short position total

Margin call equals $50,000 but is nonchargeable because $200,000 × 25% = $50,000 + 100,000 × 30% = $30,000

Total = $80,000 (minimum maintenance)

Equity is higher so although you have a call it is not chargeable.

Example #3: $100,000 equity

$100,000 long position total

$50,000 short position total

Account will have excess and therefore no margin call.

Your trade sheet's "mark to market report" contains a section called "margin figuration." This shows your total long position, total short position, total equity, or amount under minimum. Amount under minimum is your margin call.

Common Compliance Problems

1. Traders do not know their positions at all times, and sometimes close out the wrong amount.
2. Traders do not check their trade sheets for missing or extra trades.
3. A long position is sold twice.
4. A stop is entered and forgotten.

B

RESOURCES

Books

Classic Investment Theory

Bernstein, Jake. *Seasonality: Systems, Strategies, Signals.* New York: John Wiley & Sons, 1998.

Carret, Phillip L. *The Art of Speculation.* New York: John Wiley & Sons, 1997.

Cassidy, Donald L. *30 Strategies for High-Profit Investment Success.* Chicago: Dearborn Trade, 1998.

Cassidy, Donald L. *It's When You Sell That Counts.* New York: McGraw-Hill, 1997.

Coker, Daniel. *Mastering Microcaps.* New York: Bloomberg Press, 1999.

Darvas, Nicholas. *How I Made $2,000,000 in the Stock Market.* Secaucus, NJ: Carol Publishing, 1986.

Dreman, David. *Contrarian Investment Strategies: The Next Generation: Beat the Market by Going Against the Crowd.* New York: Simon & Schuster, 1998.

Fisher, Kenneth. *One Hundred Minds That Made the Market.* Business Classics, 1994.

Fisher, Philip A. *Common Stocks and Uncommon Profits.* New York: John Wiley & Sons, 1996.

Fosback, Norman. *Stock Market Logic.* Fort Lauderdale, FL: Institute for Economic Research, 1993.

Gallea, A. and, Patalon III, W. *Contrarian Investing.* Upper Saddle River, NJ: Prentice Hall, Inc., 1999.

Gardner, David, and Gardner, Tom. *The Motley Fool.* Fireside, 2001.

Good, W. and Hermansen, R. *Index Your Way to Investment Success.* Upper Saddle River, NJ: Prentice Hall, Inc., 1999.

Graham, Benjamin. *Intelligent Investor.* New York: Harper Collins, 1985.

Graja, C. and Ungar, E. *Investing in Small-Cap Stocks.* New York: Bloomberg Press, 1999.

Hagstrom, Robert. *The Warren Buffett Portfolio.* New York: John Wiley & Sons, 1999.

Hall, Alvin. *Getting Started in Stocks.* New York: John Wiley & Sons, 1997.

Investor's Business Daily. *Guide to the Markets.* New York: John Wiley & Sons, 1996.

LeFevre, Edwin. *Reminiscences of a Stock Operator.* New York: John Wiley & Sons, 1994.

Livermore, Jesse. *How to Trade in Stocks.* Traders Press, 2001.

Lowe, Janet. *Value Investing Made Easy.* New York: McGraw-Hill, 1997.

Lynch, Peter. *Beating the Street.* Fireside, 1994.

McHattie, Andrew. *Investor's Guide to Warrants.* Financial Times Management, 1996.

Murphy, Michael. *Every Investor's Guide to High-Tech Stocks and Mutual Funds.* New York: Broadway Books, 2000.

Nicholas, Joseph G. *Investing in Hedge Funds.* New York: Bloomberg Press, 1999.

Norton, Ralph. *Investing for Income.* New York: McGraw-Hill, 1999.

O'Higgins, M. and Downes, J. *Beating the Dow.* Harperbusiness, 2000.

O'Neil, William. *How to Make Money in Stocks.* New York: McGraw-Hill, 1994.

O'Shaughnessy, J. *What Works on Wall Street*. New York: McGraw-Hill, 1998.

Rothchild, John. *A Fool and His Money*. New York: John Wiley & Sons, 1998.

Scott, David L. *How Wall Street Works*. New York: McGraw-Hill, 1999.

Siegel, Jeremy. *Stocks for the Long Run*. New York: McGraw-Hill, 1998.

Taulli, Tom. *Investing in IPOs*. New York: Bloomberg Press, 1999.

Vince, Ralph. *Portfolio Management Formulas*. New York: John Wiley & Sons, 1990.

Wanetick, David. *Hot Sector Investing*. Chicago: Dearborn Trade, 1999.

Woolridge, J. and Cusatis, P. *Streetsmart Guide to Valuing a Stock: The Savvy Investor's Key to Beating the Market*. New York: McGraw-Hill, 1999.

Zweig, Martin. *Winning on Wall Street*. New York: Warner Books, 1997.

Technical Analysis

Achelis, Steven B. *Technical Analysis from A to Z*. New York: McGraw-Hill, 2000.

Arms Jr., Richard. *Arms Index*. Marketplace Books, 1996.

Arnold, Curtis M. *Timing the Market: How to Profit in Bull and Bear Markets with Technical Analysis*. New York: McGraw-Hill, 1993.

Dorsey, Thomas J. *Point and Figure Charting: The Essential Application for Forecasting and Tracking Market Prices*. New York: John Wiley & Sons, 1995.

Edwards, Robert D., and Magee, John F. *Technical Analysis of Stock Trends*. Hampton, NH: Saint Lucie Press, 2001.

Magee, John, and McDermott, Richard J. *Analyzing Bar Charts for Profits*.

Murphy, John J., and Murphy, John L. *The Visual Investor: How to Spot Market Trends*. New York: John Wiley & Sons, 1996.

Nison, Steve. *Japanese Candlestick Charting Techniques*. Upper Saddle River, NJ: Prentice Hall, Inc., 1991.

Nison, Steve. *Beyond Candlesticks: More Japanese Charting Techniques Revealed*. New York: John Wiley & Sons, 1994.

Pring, Martin J. *Technical Analysis Explained: The Successful Investor's Guide to Spotting Investment Trends and Turning Points*. New York: McGraw-Hill, 1991.

Schabacker, Richard W. *Technical Analysis and Stock Market Profits: The Real Bible of Technical Analysis.* Upper Saddle River, NJ: Financial Times and Prentice Hall, Inc., 1998.

Schwager, Jack D. *Getting Started in Technical Analysis.* New York: John Wiley & Sons, 1998.

Weinstein, Stan. *Stan Weinstein's Secrets for Profiting in Bull and Bear Markets.* New York: McGraw-Hill, 1998.

Fundamental Analysis

Copeland, Tom, Koller, Tim (Contributor), and Murrin, Jack (Contributor). *Valuation: Measuring and Managing the Value of Companies, 2d ed.* New York: John Wiley & Sons, 2000.

The Economist. *The Economist Guide to Global Economic Indicators.* New York: John Wiley & Sons, 1993.

Graham, Benjamin, and Dodd, David L. *Security Analysis.* New York: McGraw-Hill, 1996.

Mennis, Edmund A. *How the Economy Works: An Investor's Guide to Tracking the Economy.* Upper Saddle River, NJ: Prentice Hall, Inc., 1999.

Ritchie, Jr., John C. *Fundamental Analysis: A Back-to-the-Basics Investment Guide to Selecting Quality Stocks.* New York: McGraw-Hill, 1996.

Thomsett, Michael C. *Mastering Fundamental Analysis.* Chicago: Dearborn Trade, 1998.

Psychology

Douglas, Mark. *The Disciplined Trader: Developing Winning Attitudes.* Upper Saddle River, NJ: Prentice Hall, 1990.

Kindleberger, Charles P. *Manias, Panics and Crashes: A History of Financial Crises.* New York: John Wiley & Sons, 1996.

Koppel, Robert. *The Tao of Trading: Discovering a Simpler Path to Success.* Chicago: Dearborn Trade, 1998.

LeFevre, Edwin. *Reminiscences of a Stock Operator.* New York: John Wiley & Sons, 1994.

Lifson, Lawrence E. (Preface), and Geist, Richard A. *The Psychology of Investing.* New York: John Wiley & Sons, 1999.

MacKay, Charles, and Templeton, John Marks. *Extraordinary Popular Delusions and the Madness Crowds.* New York: Crown Publishing, 1995.

Patel, Alpesh B. *The Mind of a Trader: Lessons in Trading Strategy from the World's Leading Traders.* Upper Saddle River, NJ: Financial Times and Prentice Hall, Inc., 1998.

Paul, Jim, and Moynihan, Brendan. *What I Learned Losing a Million Dollars.* Infrared Pr., 1994.

Pring, Martin J. *Investment Psychology Explained: Classic Strategies to Beat the Markets.* New York: John Wiley & Sons, 1995.

Schwed, Jr., Fred. *Where Are the Customers' Yachts? or A Good Hard Look at Wall Street.* New York: John Wiley & Sons, 1995.

Financial Planning

Bresnan, Bill, and Gelb, Eric. *Getting Started in Asset Allocation.* New York: John Wiley & Sons, 1999.

Breuel, Brian H. *Staying Wealthy: Strategies for Protecting Your Assets.* New York: Bloomberg Press, 1998.

Downing, Neil. *Maximize Your Ira.* Chicago: Dearborn Press, 1998.

Gentry, F. Bruce. *The Complete Will Kit.* New York: John Wiley & Sons, 2001.

Gibson, Roger C. *Asset Allocation: Balancing Financial Risk.* New York: McGraw-Hill, 2000.

Lederman, Jess, and Klein, Robert A. (eds.). *Global Asset Allocation: Techniques for Optimizing Portfolio Management.* New York: John Wiley & Sons, 1994.

Morris, Virginia B. *Creating Retirement Income.* New York: McGraw-Hill, 1999.

Reinhardt, Carl H., Werba, Alan B., and Bowen, Jr., John J. *The Prudent Investor's Guide to Beating the Market.* Irwin Professional Pub., 1995.

Rowland, Mary. *A Commonsense Guide to Your 401(k).* New York: Bloomberg Press, 1997.

Vince, Ralph. *Portfolio Management Formulas: Mathematical Trading Methods for the Futures, Options, and Stock Markets.* New York: John Wiley & Sons, 1990.

Vince, Ralph. *The New Money Management: A Framework for Asset Allocation.* New York: John Wiley & Sons, 1995.

Media

Theoretically, only news and earnings cause a stock to move significantly. Knowledge is empowering. We recommend that all traders pursue a constant diet of reading and information gathering. Traders who have a voracious appetite for information from a variety of sources are those that ultimately prove the most successful.

Reading a wide variety of publications takes time. That is why successful traders often start their day at 7:30 A.M. (EST) to get a head start on the day's happenings, and they extend their days after the market closes to obtain after-market announcements. Information obtained pre- and postmarket coupled with reports in publications can substantially aid a trader's stock selection and trading technique. You do not make your money from 9:30 to 4:00. You make it doing your homework when the market is not open.

Internet

Please note a few of these sites are pay subscriptions.

American Banker—An excellent source of information to use for trading listed bank stocks.

Asensio—For the short seller.

Block Data—Who is the "ax"?

Bloomberg—A great site for news. Check stocks on the move premarket.

Briefing—For story stocks. A very good economic calendar for the week.

Broker Call—For analyst upgrades and downgrades.

CBS Marketwatch—One of the best sites on the Internet. Some of the best pages within CBS include Analysts' Ratings, Daily Calendar, Earnings Calendar, Economic Calendar for Week, Indications (for pre-market), Market Pulse, Movers and Shakers, Stock Splits, Stocks to Watch and Volume Report.

Daily Stocks—A new site. Rivals CBS Marketwatch for the most comprehensive on the Internet. Superb for the swing trader and investor.

Edgar-Online—Complete company reports and filings.

Financial Examiner—Excellent for the swing trader and investor.

First Call—Earnings estimates.

Fly on the Wall—Syndicate, news, analysts, great for preopen information. Very organized.

Investor Links—Ranks the financial sites.

Jagnotes—The best source of analyst information delivered premarket at 8:50 A.M., 9:05 A.M., and 9:20 A.M.

Motley Fool—A good source of intraday news.

Multex—Investor research.

Nasdaqtrader—Use for volume report to spot the "ax"; also for news about Nasdaq and trading.

Program Trading—For the trader to anticipate buy/sell programs. Very expensive.

Real Time Traders—Up-to-the-second stock alerts and analysis

Rightline.Net—The definitive source for the trader who trades stock splits.

Rumorsxpress—If you want to know the rumors on the street.

Stock Rumors—More rumors.

The Street.com—A good source of intraday news.

The whisper number—You must know the whisper number to trade earnings.

Wall Street Source—A great source of information for the serious trader. Very complete.

Magazines

Active Trader
Bloomberg Personal
Business Week
Forbes
Kiplinger's Personal Finance Magazine
Microsoft Investor
Money
On-Line Investor
Smart Money
Technical Analysis of Stocks & Commodities
Worth

Newspapers

Barron's
Investor's Business Daily
Wall Street Journal

Television

Bloomberg
CNBC
Moneyline (CNN)
Nightly Business Report (PBS)
Wall Street Week (PBS)

INDEX